David Brendan Hopes

A Sense
of the Morning

Nature Through New Eyes

Dodd, Mead & Company • New York

For my father and mother

No part of this book may be reproduced in any
form without permission in writing from the
publisher. Published by Dodd, Mead & Company,
71 Fifth Avenue, New York, New York 10003.
Manufactured in the United States of America.

First Edition

10 9 8 7 6 5 4 3 2 1

Library of Congress Cataloging in Publication Data

Hopes, David Brendan
   A Sense of the Morning.

   1. Nature—observation.   I. Title.
ISBN 0-396-09128-8

Book design and production by Eric Newman

Contents

Preface

What follows is a book of firsts. Of witness.

On the Isle of Man it was a tradition that one, leaving the house at morning, would take as his spiritual guide the first thing his eyes lit upon. How this worked I'm not sure, except in the obvious cases of the vicar or the village idiot. How would one conduct oneself if the first thing he saw were a wren or a lichenous boulder or the gray head of a seal in the tide? What if one, kneeling to tie a boot lace, saw a sexton beetle rolling his little globe of death toward the shrubbery? Would one take wing off the seacliffs with the harrying merlin? What if the cry of a strange bird caused one to stare first into the blank blue of the sky, featureless and infinite? What if a cherub with a flaming sword at the garden gate? What if a god?

Whether they are known now or not, I am convinced that there were rules for these things. On an ordinary morning I look first upon a locust tree growing from the hillside at my bedroom window. Has this made me tough and persistent? Has it clenched my grip on the turning world? Will it make me, one month hence, flower in whiteness over my gray limbs? The astonishing answer, I see now that I put it into words, is yes.

This is not a book about nature loving. Rather, it is not what you expect from a book about nature loving. If I love nature it is not because it's beautiful, though it is, but because it bears witness. Even the witness it bears is terrible and uncompromising. For every discrete fact that you can make a wise saying about, it will announce a thousand times that you will never know, never know. Like the Earth bearing witness under Buddha's finger, like the Voice from Job's Whirlwind, it utters neither scripture nor party line, but its own name over and over, an essential splendor at once demanding and incomprehensible.

What does it demand? Attention.

This is not a book about nature loving, but it is about nature and about love. If a friend says from a speeding car, nodding her head toward a patch of wood between farm houses, "I love nature," I'll mark it down in my mind never to hike with this one. It's dangerous to be enamored, even if genuinely, and yet ignorant, like a child toddling toward a crocodile, unafraid because its toothy face wears a smile. If a friend says, "I saw a pool against a wall of ice," if she buttons her top button and marches grimly toward the mountain, I've found one who loves nature as the deer loves the mountain lion, as the dry grass loves the flashfire, not for pleasantness, but for a disinterested majesty still majestic though it blasts us into atoms.

Folk legends brim with stories of animal bodies enfolding the souls of men—werewolves, the were-jaguars of Mexico, the seal-people of the British coasts. These are usually thought of as allegorical recognitions of the beast within. Most of them possess also an erotic content. The village woman falls in love with a sojourner, bears him a child, watches while he disappears into the sea one day and becomes once more a seal. A man takes a strange, cat-eyed woman to bed, wakes up to the purring of a panther. The legends are immortal because they provide one of few occasions when one may confess to a consuming and abiding love for the Other who is not God. Animals creep into the hearts of men, men into the skins of animals. We would draw closer. We would hold them in our arms.

What follows is a book of firsts—the first flower, first bird, first winter night alone on the mountain—undertaken with the faith that such things are valuable because they mark the moment when flower, bird, mountain night announce themselves to the soul, bristling and stupendous with power, almost empty of meaning. The force of such moments, like the blow of a swan's wing or a lunge into a waterfall, is immediate. Bracing and immaculate, they take our breath away without leaving us the wiser. Like Job, like Arjuna on the battlefield, we shut our mouths in awe, yet we have not been answered. What follows is a small search for meaning. It anticipates that meaning flows from the moment of annunciation gradually, circuitous and uncertain, with such slowness that the moment itself may be forgotten by the time it ripens into something usable.

What follows is a book of witness.

What follows is a history of eyes, how they start at nothing and learn the world, not from any virtue of their own but because the world wills to be seen and therefore dazzles forth eon upon eon to catch the glance. The thirteenth-century Flemish mystic John Ruusbröcc writes in *The Spiritual Espousals,* "...Christ, the wisdom of the father, has from the time of Adam spoken to all persons in an interior manner according to his divinity, addressing him with the word *See!* " So, if there are few conclusions, there is plenty of data. Of witness. If I started out wanting to provide wisdom, I ended up able only to point and cry out, *There!*

What follows is as much a treatise as I can manage on how to look at things, dared on the supposition that to look is both wisdom and salvation.

.   .   .

I thank *Audubon* magazine, *Bird Watcher's Digest, The New Yorker,* and *The Sun,* where some of this material appeared previously in one form or another.

I thank Dr. Katherine Whatley of the University of North Carolina at Asheville and Dr. Dennis J. Taylor of Hiram College for scientific advice and correction.

I thank Thomas Dolce, Nancy Graham, Dr. Carol Donley, and my Article Writing class at the University of North Carolina at Asheville for encouragement, criticism, and faithful dedication to the power of the word.

I thank Dr. David Fratus, Dr. Jeff Rackham, and Dr. Margaret Downes for seeing to it that I had time and support to do this at all.

New Eyes

Winter has been long. This is the first dawn when anyone could bear to speak of spring. The March sun rises in white flame. I wait for it to melt the rime from my car's windshield so I can drive to the mountain to hike. I could, of course, scrape it off, but the first spring hike is a ritual that a brutality might smirch. I spend time watching light climb down Town Mountain until it reaches the roofs of the valley. Bird song beats against the bedroom window. Cardinal breaks through, now and then song sparrow if he lets loose directly beneath. I watch the light climb down the mountain and try to think of the first thing I remember. This is a periodic exercise I give my mind, wanting to push the wall back, maybe to the first hour, maybe to the womb, maybe to the secret midnight of conception. It would be wonderful.

So far, however, I stop invariably at the same place—both a memory and a dream. I sit up in a crib, in a hospital room among a hundred other cribs full of sleeping children. I've awakened in the night, incapacitated by loneliness, too miserable even to cry. This part makes sense as memory. I was often sick as a child and for months spent more time in hospital wards than out.

The next part does not make the same mundane sense. I look up from the crib and see, at first, white ceiling tiles peppered with black soundproofing dots. I blink, open my eyes, and the ceiling has turned into its negative, white flecks on black.

No. I see now. The ceiling has disappeared along with the roof and the steel smog over Cleveland, and I sit at the plinth of a black sky shot with stars.

❦

A dreaming man is vulnerable. The campfire dies. Moon sinks in a tangle of thorns. A day bird screams once from her nest until slithering coils shut her throat. The panther sniffs the dreamer's hair, moves on—or crouches, watching. The she-wolf's eyes burn from the shadow of the forest. In the dream, worse things still stalk out on glittering claws. Caught between two midnights, he dreams on. He pushes into the next wilderness, the next horror, waiting for the dark road to break into the open, where he can run, or turn and fight.

❦

Imagine this: You are an interstellar voyager. You left Earth when you were very young. You've lost count of the days in which your world has been a cylinder of hybrid metals—silent, cold, unimaginably swift, progressing imperceptibly through the net of stars. But one morning you wake—not quite wake, but hover between dream and waking—with a scent in your nostrils, wet and dark, sweet and bitter, as motionless as stone, as quick as rain. Automatically your mind reaches back, probing, struggling for the remembrance. Then you have it. You wake with a sense of the morning, starting straight up as you did as a child, ready for the light like saffron in your window. No. Metal and silence and starlight. But you know there is a possession now, something internal and therefore permanent, some weightless baggage worth the rest of your cargo, whatever it is: that sense-memory, that knot in the nerves you carry forever, the pearl called Home.

4

❦

Imagine this: After troubled sleep you wake. You survey your little space, to determine why you are no longer comfortable, no longer at home. You see at last that all is changed. You are an old bird in a new tree. You must adjust.

Night complexities dissolve into a geometry of dew sparkling from the high twigs; simple, you think, incalculably pure and near. You take a moment to see that some invisible power has burned away habitual perception. What was green stands blazing emerald. The heights arc into the sky; the depths plunge to the bottom of the world. You have been given new eyes. You don't remember asking, or having had the wisdom to ask, but still they sizzle in your sockets like infant stars.

A locust tree leans against your window. It always has. But, as in a naïve and perfect painting of Eden, it wears now leaf and blossom and fruit at once. Freed from the labor of distinguishing potential from actuality, history from present moment, the possible from the longed-for, you simultaneously hunger and feed. White crescent moons of flowers perfume the air. Wing, keel, standard, stigma, anther stand forth, each hair and filament etched in fire.

O Locust Tree! you cry, believing for the first time that it will hear.

On ordinary mornings, a cardinal sings from the locust's top branch. If he did now, the window would burst and the walls reverberate with red thunder, the roof explode like paper on a bonfire.

Imagine especially this: Your lover lies on the bed beside you, changed, almost unrecognizable for beauty and solemnity and delight. Human, of course, but like the locust tree, actual and potential in one instant, spring and full summer, golden autumn, winter a white sleep before thaw. The fluttering of a lover's eyelid makes a further morning, morning upon morning downward through the kingdoms of the brain.

You perceive suddenly the immensity of the sacrifice. Your lover's hand on the white sheet possesses carbon, oxygen, calcium, nitrogen, iron, magnesium, the finger brightened by a gold ring. Now, only the hydrogen bound to the waters of that body is primal matter. At the creation of things was hydrogen, the One. To give that hand indispensable carbon, a star burns through six billion years of hydrogen, fusing hydrogen nuclei into helium, fusing clustered helium nuclei into carbon, four times three a trillion-fold each second.

Merely huge stars unable to burn carbon die then, flickering into cold ghosts freezing their dead worlds around them. Supergiants capable of carbon fusion collapse, re-ignite by the pressure of compression, fuse their nuclei into oxygen. Having burnt their oxygen, they once again collapse, re-ignite, burn sodium, collapse, re-ignite, whirling through terrible cycles of fusion and collapse and resurrection on up to iron. The star finally explodes or shucks its layers in a burning Catherine wheel. Its matter scatters through the universe to be sucked up by infant planets: at last ours, this Earth, after who knows how many generations of suns, gathering the jetsam of vanished worlds that your love might wake at morning.

Nor is that all. Light elements between helium and carbon, too complex to be fully elemental, too fragile for the roaring furnace, arise from the caress of cosmic rays, helium nuclei snatching protons out of emptiness.

For elements beyond iron, not even the crucible of a star suffices. The light of the luminous bedroom clock and the gold of the ring that binds you are born of a supernova, an exploding gigantic sun in which incomprehensible force and unimaginable resistance meet head-on and, despite the cocktail-party conundrum, do not stalemate but flower into the principal cataclysm of created worlds. There is nothing comparable. To be within a billion miles is to be snuffed out in terrible splendor. Supernovae outshine galaxies—briefly, but for such glory, briefly is enough. Heavy elements hurl outward from the fading wreck. They fall into suns, onto the frozen faces of dead planets. They rain into the trencher of the newborn Earth, so that four billion years later they might course through the blood, eddy in and out with the breath.

Tell this to a suicide, if he gives you time.

Answer this when the priest asks, "Who made you?"

❦

Years ago I sat in a seminar room in Baltimore, too young to be a graduate student, homesick, lonely, and unready, wondering if I could really be as stupid as everyone and every incident made me feel. Professors discoursed brilliantly; my colleagues answered their questions, laughed at their quips with laugh-track enthusiasm, while I sank deeper each day. That it is now funny is a gift of time.

Late afternoons, a mockingbird beat to the lilac shrub outside the classroom window. He waited for the branch to stop quivering and began to sing, with infinite liquid invention, with a satiric wit that mocked sweetly, I imagined, the drone of erudition from the room. I couldn't have been the only one hearing him, but perhaps I was the only one *needing* to hear him. I listened, eyes narrowed the way eyes narrow when the soul listens. The first time, I believed he was a mistake. The second time, too good to be true. As he arrived like clockwork one afternoon upon another, I began to think of him as special grace. He gave me peace. What was that little room? A bird from the middle of the blue serenaded me, and for the first time it was absolutely necessary for me to listen. Like Siegfried, I had bathed in dragon's blood and fathomed every note.

It didn't hurt that the course was Romantic Poets, and one afternoon we must have considered Keats's nightingale, doing for him what my mockingbird did for me—opening the casement window onto the foam of perilous seas in faery lands forlorn.

The remarkable thing was that I forgot the mockingbird from day to day, and when afternoon class passed its first hour his advent on the lilac bush was ever a fresh delight, an innovation, a gift unheralded.

❦

Day upon day, winter persists. Like those bad old times under the ice, spring comes by the calendar, yet silent, motionless. New Hampshire's Squamscott River is a plain of ice. Trees on its bank glitter, glass-encased, wind banging their frozen branches into hollow music.

I hear the other sound twice before I believe my ears and look. It's the rattle of kingfishers. Across the stone river a pair of kingfishers scream and hover, shaking the willow-wrecks into rainbow when they land. Too soon. The river—the world—lies frozen. There's nothing to eat. Fish the ice, my loves.

I call aloud to them *too soon!*, but they aren't listening. Can't dive through ice. I close my eyes and see them starving, their blue going out like snuffed flame. I stand at the edge of the ice calling *too soon* until cars pass and shame me away.

That night I dream of kingfishers. They hover over a river of crystal lying motionless, pure and silent, a plain of living ice. They scream and hover. Sapphires with the sun behind them. Finally they pull their jewel wings back and dive. Again and again they rise, pause, thunderbolt onto the river with their diamond beaks, shearing, hammering, spraying shattered crystal around them. Up and down, inexhaustable as gods.

I wake from the dream too early, still in the grip of night. I listen for what woke me. A song. A roaring. The window tells me it's rain—not just rain, a torrent, a cloudburst. Black sheets of water hurl from the roof, falling too fast for the ice in the gutters to give and let it be carried away. Under the clap of rain sounds the rifle-shot of river ices cracking, heaving like mountains in a time-lapse movie of Creation. The Squamscott gathers itself, swirls to the sea.

Spring.

An iron fist shatters the ice. I dress, run to the river, watch the kingfishers dive, thunder up laden with fish.

❦

Homo sapiens is a tropical African species. Our first winters were rainy, followed by dry summers, spells of profound aridity that occasionally lasted for centuries, driving us down from the withering trees onto the leopard-haunted veldt. Some of us, to escape the drought, or simply out of curiosity, walked north, where glaciers lay across Europe and Siberia and joined the Old World to the New. What we made of that Ur-winter is difficult now to know, but some of us must have been intrigued. We moved into the deeper north, wearing the skins of beasts, letting our color change to the color of the snow and the pale tundra flowers, stopping only when the frozen continents came to an end.

·   ·   ·

Someone must bear witness, though all that can be said is a gnomic first-of-spring *haiku,* a single phrase like the label of a snapshot in an album, "Kingfishers over frozen river."

❦

I sit reading against an osier bush in Oakwood Cemetery in Syracuse. I've sat so long and still that the bush's hermit thrush forgets I'm here. Dusk falls; he begins to sing. I've heard thrushes, but never before ten inches from my ear. Like a river of bells, he flows and chimes at once. Like an instrument, he seems never to need breath. He gurgles a line, halts, reconsiders, alters the passage, sings it through twice to make it right, launches into variations at once florid and austere, so sweet and loud that I want to say, with some sickly Romantic poet, it is too much to bear. But I bear it, book dropped face-down on the grass. Venus shines out and woodthrush launches from his branch to hunt. He pauses, stares at me, the beads of eyes asking what I can present him in return. The answer is *nothing*.
Or this.

My cousin Diane, pregnant with her first child, walked daily along the Atlantic. The pregnancy was difficult, her military husband on assignment far away, and each day opened a renewed struggle to keep her spirit quick and the child alive. On her beach walks she began to collect fragments from the sand. This became an obsession, and soon she had a box of hard, serrated remembrances. At length someone asked her why she was collecting shark teeth. Though she hadn't known they were shark teeth, the answer was clear and direct. They were a symbol of endurance. Look on a shark's tooth. Nowhere will you see etched, "I am a symbol of endurance." It isn't necessary. Consider the abysses, the famines and dangers. Consider the baffles of accident through which they floated to my cousin's feet on the wild shore. She gathered her shark teeth, and the child was born. Around her neck to this day a black, jagged tooth hangs from a golden chain, where some wear a cross for the same reason.

. . .

One's deepest intuition is that the world is holy. Whether this is subliminal apprehension of the majesty of God or subliminal compensation for the absence of God does not, ultimately, matter. A buttress raised by faith and a buttress raised by desperate will both hold the wall up.

After you've spent a certain time gleaning in libraries and from the hearts of your neighbors, in order to learn any worthwhile thing at all you must let go. You must relinquish pride in whatever you think makes you human. Yes, it is glory to be human, but it is not infinity, not even the whole of one small blue planet.

You must hike past the end of the road, for while you're on the road you're still in control. Adam made it; Adam's smell pervades it. You must, as Ezekiel says, go up into the gaps. You hike past the farthest point you've known before. Of course it is beautiful, but that's not why you go. It may be the first step you've ever taken beyond, and if so you are very lucky.

Go hungry if you can.

Deep in winter, after many frosts and snows, I've found clusters of wild grapes on the forest floor, cold but edible and sweet. Explain that.

I know, Elisha was fed by ravens. But he saw them coming. He could say, "The ravens fed me." I don't know whom to thank. Or why.

Pass the end of the road. Wait for a summons. Go in love and dread. If you were a saint you would go barefoot, binoculars held before you like a monk's begging bowl, hungry for something to be dropped in.

Moral philosopher William Paley crossing the heath strikes his foot against stone and allows himself to suppose it lay dully and accidentally there forever. William Paley crossing the heath strikes his foot against a watch and insists he has found order, agency, will, intelligence, the God-deducing artifice.

The algae in the canyons of the stone, its silica fleck from the furnace of a star, lifts unanswerable contradiction.

.   .   .

A stone is witness. It implies the cosmos as the watch implies a watchmaker. Its history makes the watch the briefest of ephemera in comparison. Pass the road's end. Gather stones. Stuff your pockets with the passions of a billion years. One from the valleys of the moon. One from the bottom of the Ur-sea. One spilled from Africa when it slammed into the coast of North America and heaved up the mountains where I write.

I have a book with a picture of a mottled stone in it, and under the picture a caption reads, "Meteorite suspected of having come from Mars." There are people one suspects of coming from Mars, but a *rock*? The next step is for these things to amaze us beyond words.

Find where the Martian rock fell. Stand there with your arms open, waiting.

Start where the road ends.

In 1802 the same William Paley succumbs to an ecstasy of hopefulness and naïvety, writing in "Natural Theology, or the Evidences of the Existence and Attributes of the Deity, Collected from the Appearance of Nature":

> ...It is a happy world after all. The air, the earth, the water teem with delighted existence. In a spring noon, or a summer evening, on whichever side I turn my eyes, myriads of happy beings crowd my view....Swarms of newborn *flies* are trying their pinions in the air. Their sportive motions, their wanton mazes, their gratuitous activity, their continual change of place without use or purpose, testify their joy, and the exultation which they feel in their lately discovered faculties....Other species are *running about* with an alacrity in their motions which carries with it every mark of pleasure.

For eight generations, Paley's sanguineness must have provoked howls of derision from the scientific community. Would it now? I watch nature specials on public television that use but parsimoniously those subjective words *pleasure* and *enjoy* and *beautiful* but that permit in their photography a hue of rapture falling little short of Paley's, that employ scientific experts whose sobriety endures until, explaining birdsong or whalesong, they admit—at the last possible instant, as though hoping their flightier viewers had already turned to less provocative amusements—that after territory and mating and warning are accounted for, these creatures sing for pure delight.

It has taken until this century for science to admit that it is itself a mythology. Remember that the factuality of myth is wholly irrelevant. What counts is its beauty; and the myth that splits the atom in the rose's thorn, that times the beat of the pulsar, is beauty to break the heart. I know this because when I was young and ferocious, I believed that some things were true and others false. Such faith made me monstrous. I've changed my tune. I say, *Some things are beautiful....*

I've never known if it's humanity we seek in wilderness, or something to take the place of humanity. The doe and her fawn, the trout balanced in bright water like a compass needle thralled by true north, are not identical to oneself, but we are nevertheless allies, members of the same party. I don't mean this in a purely ecological sense. I want to say that we are connected spiritually, but that is hardly more specific, and bound to irritate those to whom matters of the spirit are an embarrassment. Let's say this: Overflowings of the same inexhaustible fountain, we long for each other with the longing of separated twins. The hemoglobin in the whale's blood warbles to the hemoglobin in mine; both cry out to the star that forged their iron in convulsions of a vanished dispensation. We are children of the same House, the first House, and only.

It is March, a charmed time for me and skunks. The Blue Ridge Parkway has been closed for weeks, because ice storms followed by gale-force winds destroyed trees, sent limbs and trunks and hillsides crashing down so that the road and most of the forest paths lie impassable. I try, though. I climb over hulks of poplars shattered like kindling, over tangles of laurel uprooted like a pulled and tossed-aside weed. It takes me seven hours to go as far as I could go in four in

November. Along the paths, six-foot branches were driven into the ground like javelins. To have been in the forest when the wind came on the tail of the ice would have been to die.

Or so I say, dramatically, seeing nary a corpse amid the kindling.

At evening, tired, I make my way down. Not one other human soul disturbs the mountain, though the day shines blue and cool. The road is as deserted and strewn with shattered lumber as a highway after Armageddon. Shadows grow long. The moon climbs invisibly behind the blue range eastward. I break from the cover of the forest and walk maybe fifteen feet before stopping dead. A skunk forages on the roadside, not more than a running long jump away. It's a large male, creamy white in two thick bands along his back, black only at dead center, so pale that I'm not sure he's skunk until he faces me with that unmistakable sad clown mask. I watch a long time. I'm downward of a considerable wind, and his vision is worse than mine. When I tire of watching I have to shout, "Skunk, let me pass!," surprising a skunk being a very bad idea. He swivels to keep a beady eye on me but continues foraging. I skitter by, knowing who is the master of the situation.

Skunks are Mustelidae, a family that includes weasels, fishers, otters, ferrets, badgers, and that beast-Shiva, the wolverine. The skunk is one of the three or four most familiar wild animals in North America, and yet certain things about it remain all but unknown. First, like us it does not stink if it is happy. Second, it is a creature of serenity perturbable only by the most extreme provocation, and hence an example to us all. Third, it sings.

One March evening long ago I heard a skunk sing for the first time. I walked by starlight down Udall Road in Hiram, Ohio, when I heard her in the field between me and the forest. I watched her waddle from the shadow of the trees, to the road, across the road not more than six feet away, the whole time mumbling and twittering to herself like someone deep in thought.

Central to the experience was the odd sense of having encountered her before—not just some skunk on some road, but *her*. I've never shied from the anthropomorphic, and I wallow in it now: Something in her lack of either skittishness or aggression let me assume a shared and not-quite-forgotten moment of calm acceptance.

The next day, wanting that intensity of experience again, I skipped classes and fought through the encircling brambles into the valley of Silver Creek. I moved north on the high ridge between Udall Road and the stream. Involved in my thoughts, I passed through an undifferentiated gray wood, gray trunks of generic trees, gray sky, gray of last year's foliage on the forest floor.

A mile out, on the highest point of the ridge, I heard the skunk. She summoned me into the world like the sudden focusing of a lens. The sky had not been gray, but serene early-spring ice blue. The trees wore no gray at all, though I looked hard, wanting to justify the misty perceptions of the past mile. The silvery steel of the beeches came nearest. The rest shone brown and red-brown and white and silver and black and red-black, animated by the Jacob's-laddering of nuthatches easing down and creepers scrambling up.

I stood within thirty feet of the skunk, then moved closer, to a log to sit and watch. She was building a nest against a fallen maple on the ridgepole of the forest, close to water, far from the farm dogs, high, dry, riddled with light. What I had heard the night before as mumbling and chuckling was now clearly singing. The skunk sang as she built her nest.

The song was without meter. It had rhythm, I suppose, but one as complex and random as rainfall, and I couldn't follow it. The pitches wandered and rambled, the sound of water falling from stone to stone.

Of course she knew I was there. She had invited me.

Once she stood on her hind feet and balanced with her front paws resting on my log. Her small weight changed the alignment of the wood. She stared at me, silent for the moment, then dropped onto all fours and went about her business, which was, I see now, as much singing as building.

I didn't ask myself until much later what I would have done had she come nearer. I hope I wouldn't have disgraced my species. She scuffled and rooted in the woods, and sang.

·   ·   ·

A mystic will tell you that the experience of the vision is the meaning of the vision. I am impatient with that sort of explanation, which is no explanation at all. I say. "It's a cheat! A casuistry!"

The Blue Ridge answers, "Welcome to Planet Earth."

All earthly matters are cheats and casuistries if we insist on an *apparent* consistency, if we look frantically in geology or physics or religion for the appearance of continuity. Consistency is a concept at odds with the true continuity of things, which is a pattern of change too vast and radiant for human theory to encompass. Rocks battered here by fire were battered there by flood. Yesterday's immutable atom is today's fleeting quantum. God does not say the same thing on Sinai as He does in Galilee.

Yet the universe is not random. There is a consistent message. It is not *understand* but *see;* not *know* but *love.*

What does the shark's tooth sing? What the skunk and the mockingbird? I would reveal it if I knew, if I weren't resigned to the fact that the singing itself is the message of the song.

The locust wears starfire at morning. A hair of the beloved is hieroglyphed with histories of the convulsions of suns. The message? Simply *behold.*

The hills break forth into singing. The trees of the field clap their hands. If you ask *Why?* you have missed the point completely.

It's difficult to think of these things long, but thought of they will be, by their insistence. Like Jacob wrestling with the angel, they will not let us go until we bless them.

How to bless them? Point and cry out.

I shout to the foraging skunk, "Let me pass!"
He says, "Have you seen me and remembered?"
"Yes."
"Pass then. And be quick."

Past Lives

A while back I earned my living as the sort of naturalist who leads people through the forest, telling them what flutters, scurries, photosynthesizes around them. This is called being an "interpretive naturalist," though at the time I would have described it as "scrambling for a job." To obtain this position one had to take a civil-service exam that asked questions like "Would you put vertical stripes or bright-colored blotches on the costume of an actor to make him look taller?" Part of the reason I don't attack bureaucracy with greater violence than I do is that it usually works in my favor. I knew the answer and could tell a tortoise from a mad dog, so I got the job. I'd had no training but was a demon in the forest, greeting what screamed or bloomed around with the familiarity of a cousin at a family reunion.

My first employer in this capacity was the Akron, Ohio, Parks and Recreation Department, which hauled urban and suburban kids to my park in a bus driven by a handsome Latino named Lou. Lou wore a heavy gold chain and a medallion as bright as the moon in the black hair of his chest. This made me admire what I took as the

Catholic emancipation of the body, foreign to the T-shirted and strictly underweared Protestants I'd known all my life.

Lou's expression when he pulled up told me how the day was going to go. If he laughed and joked, it would be an easy day filled with well-behaved and thoroughly admonished kids grateful for an outing. If Lou arrived scowling—well, to adapt Tolstoi's comment about families, good days were just good days, while every disaster dwells in memory with appalling uniqueness.

There was David, a fourteen-year-old neighborhood kid who scattered my line of forest walkers with his dirt bike until one day I offered him half my sandwich, after which he couldn't be pried from my side until quitting time, displaying a devotion that, though quieter than the dirt bike, was scarcely less nerve-racking. No one has adored me since with quite the same ferocity, and I wish I'd appreciated it at the time.

There was Margaret, my co-worker, placed there by some unwonted levity of bureaucracy, who hated the outdoors and wore nylons to hike along through the brambly wild; who presided over lunchtime like a Dickensian orphanage-keeper, hoarding the sandwiches until they could be doled out according to a scale of deservedness fathomed only by herself.

There were the suburban kids bored out of their minds by the effort to appear uninterested. Nothing could be done for them. Go back to the mall and set this down as a day wasted.

There were the ghetto kids terrified by each sound, each wave of the branch. Them I could help by saying, "What's the worst it could be?" and when they went through the possibilities, even when they included bears and Dracula, they understood that we were the most fearsome beings in the valley.

I took them from the path to see a chestnut sprouting from a stump dead when their grandfathers were boys. I made them wade in the Cuyahoga River miles above where it took fire in the flats of Cleveland to feel living waters at their knees, to see kingfishers zoom to their dinners at eye level. Ten-pound carp dreadnoughted in the deep at the center, grown to dull gold leviathans after having been flushed from the garden pools of Cuyahoga Falls or down the toilets of Akron. I held out the long muscle of the garter snake, to let the boldest of them touch.

I'd never seen people so frightened before. Green made them uneasy. The fluttering of leaves or the chattering of squirrels edged them toward panic. An open space sent them scurrying to the shadows. When I brought them to the river to wade they huddled on the shore, touching their toes gingerly to the surface, holding themselves and shivering. Anything I told them of the world was news.

See here? A mitre of Jack-in-the-pulpit seed, phallic and provocative in the green of high summer.

That? The wallop of the pileated woodpecker. Crow-sized, fire-headed, screaming like a madwoman lost in the woods. Cousin to the ghostly ivory-billed, who is like Arthur and Elijah much rumored but returns finally only at the end of time.

That? Spiderwort, cool blue on a day that blazes with heat over the treetops. I want to pluck it and gobble it down, still covered with morning dew. I confide this desire to my charges, and they say *Eeewwwww.*

I lead them down a path cut for a power line. The path connects the river with the power station downtown, a distance of two miles. Wild hollyhocks bloom on all sides, droning with bees. Sweet pea kisses our ankles. I don't tell them what I see here in the morning, before the bus arrives: bums, asleep, hung over, once in a while dead. To tell the dead from the dead drunk you must touch. Kick and yell if after a touch you are still uncertain.

I pluck a leaf of a shining, oily-green vine, hold it aloft, and say, "Does anyone know what *this* is?" and when the answer, poison ivy, is finally revealed, wait for the squeal, "But you have it in your *hand*." I don't know if I'm immune or not. I was then, because I insisted on it, for the glory of that moment.

A tame raccoon put in an appearance when it suited his ends, these ends being bits of leftover lunch. If we passed in the morning he ignored us. If it was after noon, he launched into his act, knowing that Margaret had doled out the sandwiches and dry apples. The children could touch him if they dared, but only on the paws, and only in the act of handing him food. It was irresponsible for me to let this go on, raccoons being formidable fighters able to take on twice their weight in dogs; but I saw as my major task to get children comfortable with nature, and flapping friendly animals away with my T-shirt sent the wrong message. My teenage friend David called the 'coon Debbie, though he was certainly a wily old boar, a giant the size of a collie, who one day treated a transfixed but oddly unhorrified group of children to the disembowlment of a dog that yapped an inch too close. The yellow mongrel died on the path in front of us. The children peered at the spectacle as at a microscope slide or an exhibit in a museum. Later I came to think of this attitude as the correct one.

Not one of them said a word while getting back on the bus. Lou raised his eyebrows in thanks for my having sent them back subdued.

That night I received a phone call from a furious parent who believed I'd staged the whole episode.

Inevitably—maybe fearing I could say anything and he wouldn't know better—someone asked how I knew the names and histories of wild things. Sometimes I could admit that so-and-so told me or that I read it in a book. More often I didn't know how I knew, couldn't remember not knowing.

When does one first know? A robin is a robin; it's at once a fact and a birthright. Was it ever possible to confuse sycamore and beech? At what hour did one notice the high and subtle flowers of the oak? I could claim these details as prenatal heritage with a clean conscience. Well within the age of reason I remember *just knowing* a creature the first time I ever set eyes on it. I believe this is common to the race. We are like maidens in fairy tales, drugged and dragon-harried, who recognize our true-loves because they are the ones who appear at the hour of our need.

Hiking scruffy urban woods, I heard kicking and scrabbling in dry leaves, and I knew it was the towhee. Knew the word. Knew this is where the bird would be, though I'd never seen it, knew no one as interested in such things as I who could have told me.

I said "trillium" to myself the first time I encountered its blooms littering the wood floor. I'd named the thing secretly and uniquely and felt a thrill of coincidence when I learned that "trillium" really was its name. Again and again I knew things I shouldn't have, as though creation had set out to confirm me as a Platonist before puberty. One might say I had read these things in a book and recalled them upon visual confirmation. I say not, though the point is unprovable.

These things cannot be spoken of outside of the context of literature, or of the sort of friendship in which anything can be said because everything is forgotten. This is not how a scientist works, but rather a shortcut given to the artist, whose labor must be expended on something beyond purely finding out.

I cherish, for its revelation about the nature of my commitment to the wild, the first time it occurred to me to go looking for birds, rather than just keeping alert to what might be around. I lived in Hiram, Ohio, where my roommate rose with the sun each spring morning to go birding, and though I made fun of his dedication, one dawn I crept out behind him. I took my gigantic binoculars (hugeness in binoculars indicated ornithological seriousness then, just as smallness does now) to Maddy's Pond, at the edge of the college playing fields. There, in the space of twenty minutes, I saw the myrtle warbler, the green heron, and several pairs of bluebirds nesting in trees that overhung the water, that fluttered out periodically to gather insects, the shocking blueness of their backs stark over the jade green of the miraculous waters. I sat back in the ferns as one stricken. The experience filled me with lasting, overwhelming hunger, a longing that was not for understanding, but like the pure greed of a miser, for simply *more*.

Ezra Pound writes, "What thou lovest well remains to thee." I add a corrollary: "What thou lovest well awaits thee," whispering its name in the wild wood so you hear before you see. I have evidence to conclude we know the countenance, the smell, the certain curve of things that we will love long before we encounter them.

Sometimes the encounter is aborted. We take the wrong path. We're cold and tired, and we turn homeward. But there remains a jag in our hearts, a lingering feeling of incompleteness. Certain hilltops and seashores call us because we have not witnessed what they mean for us to witness. Don't take my word for this. Question your bones.

In one unique passage of necessary folly, I quit graduate school to live on a commune in the horsey and rolling Maryland countryside. This was no gaggle of granola fantasticks gathered together for a weekend under the stars. The commune had been founded in 1949 by literacy missionaries; it was housed in a mansion that once belonged to a U.S. senator; our neighbors on one side were the Calverts, of Maryland's founding family, and on the other the great opera star Rosa Ponsell.

My job was to serve as community naturalist. Compared with Nature Day Camp in Akron, the situation seemed luxurious. The duties were vague, in keeping with the do-your-own-thing '70s but centered on giving visitors and residents "a sense of the natural world." This they already possessed, so I did my work as I had before, pointing out birds and flowers, relating their habits or medicinal properties when I knew them. Oddly, I was never asked these things. If I didn't volunteer the information, it remained embedded in the mystery. I put it down to the eldest member's being a devout Quaker, to whom the thing unsaid was the thing made mighty.

The commune tried to grow its own food and succeeded with fruits and vegetables. Mulberries overhung Honey Brook. Strawberries clung to the southern hill, waiting to be picked by Marian, the community nurse, who'd left the war zones of Vietnam to harvest here in the morning light. If you picked with her, you went on down the rows until you heard her, hoisting herself up from her knees, confide to the strawberry vines, "Well, too much is enough." Intensive organic gardening raised crops all year, tough roots growing even in winter between banks of radiating compost. Dick, Quaker sage and former agricultural missionary to China, mustered the garden crews with an efficiency that left room for inspiration. All that summer, the bean rows veered abruptly to the north, because where they would have run stood a single noble cardinal flower that he would not let be plowed over.

.　　　.　　　.

24

At midsummer one of my co-workers came to my room carrying a jar covered by a cloth. He said, "Here. You're the person who would appreicate this."

Inside the jar coiled a young milk snake, in wheat and cream checkerboard as bright as Eden. It poured into my hand, where, instead of diving for the open door, it curled contentedly, as though I were a rock set in the sun to warm it.

While I lived at the commune I dreamed in threes before morning. Three lights. Three beasts. Three strange loves. Gradually I perceived myself *hearing* in threes. Easing awake, I renewed relations with the Carolina wren beneath my window in the garden house, whooping with his little claws tight on a mimosa twig, many times louder and more gallant than size would seem to allow.

The commune folk told me the wren cried *Rise and shine! Rise and shine!,* but I found in him such vehemence I heard *Go to hell! Go to hell!,* the emphasis, like a country preacher's, migrating through the syllables, though ever first on the first.

Years of listening provide the observation of regional, or perhaps individual, variations. The wren that nested under my eaves in Hominy Valley, North Carolina, roared *taDAda taDAda,* in moments of extreme ardor flinging himself into the driveway sycamore to ring out amphibrachs of incomparable loudness and purity.

Besides boldness, the wren possesses several qualities I prize in humans. He is not too proud. He builds in the scruffy tangles by the driveway, leaving lordly oak and tulip to others. He is valiant. I've watched the she-wren scan from the eaves of my porch for the neighbor's taffy cat, hopping from one stick foot to the other in anticipation, then powerdive, rattling like a snake when the poor beast blunders in range. He is mechanical. I go to my car at morning; he flutters out from under it, as if caught tinkering with the joints and shafts. Most of all, he is loyal. He and his mate stay the winter, *hammerklaviering* the same threes through sleet and blizzard after the rest of the world has lightwinged south.

Two pairs of wrens dwelt within bellowing distance of my bed on the commune, one in an old log pile under my window, another in the raspberry patch that gleamed in the light of the open beyond encircling conifers.

Twice a day in prime yield weather the berries needed picking, and working the wrens' row was a test of mettle. You wondered when you'd be startled witless by a ball of bird fury exploding inches from your face. Nor could any accommodation be reached, as critical distance altered with each picking. Sometimes you could pluck berries overhanging the nest like old-fashioned light fixtures. At other times the birds met you, tails bobbing with incipient battle-fury, at the edge of the garden. Surely nobody is afraid of wren, yet for six feet on either side of the nest hung raspberries, bursting ripe, untouched.

❧

"Naturalist" was the most satisfying job I ever had, and when I ask myself why I gave it up, I realize it had to do with the division between what one would and what one ought.

Another way of saying that is to observe that one's love may be genuine, but the expression inappropriate. I am a writer; I grew up sure to be a scientist.

What kind of scientist changed from year to year. After reading Roy Chapman Andrews I loved dinosaurs fiercely, jealously, obsessively. Another boy's playing with my plastic pterosaur drove me wild; the nightmare wings belonged in my hands only. Typical of any first passion, I have never completely recovered. To this day I'd cross the street to see the pope or the Mona Lisa but would crawl on hands and knees through bog and glacial moraine for a really hideous fossil.

I read a boy's book of great archeological discoveries—Carter in Egypt, Schliemann in Troy, Evans at Knossos—and peopled my days with dead kings and golden empires.

Someone bought me a Golden Book of the Solar System, over which I pored in the first grade to the detriment of all other studies. I was spared the consequences of going intellectually AWOL by the understanding of my teacher, Mrs. Rock, whom I mention by name to thank her for wisdom and latitude that set young curiosity on a free path.

For her sake I should have saved a corner of my heart for geology, though I never quite did, always preferring what squirmed, screamed, or flew, or that once had done so.

The first mentionable money I had for my own was ten dollars, bequeathed by an expiring ancestor. My parents insisted on banking half—"for college," the sweet naïvete of that striking me only now—but let me have the rest to spend as I wished. I knew what I wanted. They insisted I wait and "think about it," but when at last they drove me downtown, I bought what I would have bought the instant they put the money in my hands: five Golden Book nature guides, which one could get for a buck each then: Birds, Mammals, Reptiles and Amphibians, Insects, The Seashore. I read them, memorized them, recall the illustrations in detail now even though the books themselves have been lost for twenty years.

A friend got a chemistry set for Christmas; for six months we were mad scientists, mixing unspeakable brews and dipping crickets into them to see what happened, in a parody of scientific experimentation. If our class had a science club, I was president of it. I saved my pennies and bought a gas-blue volume called *The Human Body,* from which could be learned delicious words like *endocrine* and *medulla oblongata.*

I practiced big words to say in church, where such show-offiness was acceptable so long as you kept a sense of proportion. I corrected the teachers in science class, and they could say little back, as I was right.

Yet it wasn't actually science that interested me. I wouldn't have had the vocabulary to express it, but the fascination was aesthetic rather than scientific. I acted like a scientist because it was a beautiful thing to do; and in a time when boys weren't sent to dance class or given piano lessons or encouraged to draw anything but cars and cowboys, in the near–post-*Sputnik* era when art was deemphasized for the sake of science, it was the one acceptable expression of the aesthetic impulse. Some of us played scientist because the role, so far as we could tell, was the lead.

I could have continued to play scientist. I wouldn't have been a very good one, though with my stunned appreciation of showy scientific discovery perhaps I could have been a useful science teacher. Eventually circumstance showed me a more direct route to the desire of my heart. Creation opens to eyes other than—sometimes superior to—the burning spear of the microscope.

For me, science was the doorstep into art. For some, the sequence is reversed.

The impulse of science and the impulse of art are at first indivisible, one unified longing for the things of the world. I didn't understand this as a child, of course, and approach understanding now only after opening a suitcase full of old science-fair prizes and citations for excellence in college biology, wondering how that road became the one I tread now. There was but one road, the King's Highway, which split on the day I realized I could not know everything.

I want to draw a distinction. I want to point to the hover of dragonflies over still water and say, "Science regards the dancer, poetry the dance." But the opposite could be asserted with equal accuracy. I want to say, "Science uses; art rejoices," but I keep silent, knowing that what is necessary in the world is power—for beauty and goodness, it is to be hoped, but power nevertheless. I'd use the splendor of the world in an instant if I could really ensnare it with words.

Maybe I can, and grace protects creation by preserving my innocence.

I lecture to my classes at the University of North Carolina at Asheville that science and art are one impulse, the blue and the red of a single ray of white light, hoping it's true, unwilling to have lost anything by having chosen between them.

❧

I clearly remember first becoming aware of both art and science as material removed from the background noise of existence, and of their reconcilable but peculiar properties, and that it happened in one instant.

28

Born with pulmonary stenosis, I spent part of my childhood visiting doctors. At the time I write of now I was four years old, a fact known only from clippings of the event that our hometown newspaper found somehow featureworthy. I felt older, or rather felt then exactly as now, a phenomenon that's probably common to the race but nevertheless amazing to me.

Generally I played in the waiting rooms while my parents consulted with the cardiologist over electrocardiogram readouts. For two or three years I was America's most thorough and reluctant devourer of *Highlights for Children* magazine.

On the wall of all medical waiting rooms then hung reproductions of Impressionist landscapes, on the theory, I suppose, that they broadcast serenity. Otherwise this particular office had little to recommend it to a boy: a few games with pieces missing and that you couldn't play by yourself anyway, a Children's Bible with a vivid Moses-wielding-the-tablets cover but an interior crayoned over by urchins younger or less well-brought-up than oneself, a receptionist who'd talk for a while but insisted eventually on getting back to work.

After riffling through the picture magazines, nervous energy led me to the Impressionist reproduction on the peach-colored wall. Once my eyes connected, they would not be torn away. The painting represented how things look, but not really. You could tell it was meant to be a river and overarching trees, but not quite that, not *just* that. Why the ambiguity? Why did it look so much like what anyone would see standing on the same spot, and yet not, as though at the last instant it willed itself into something irreproducible? I didn't have the words, but I had the thoughts. The painting disturbed me. It was something grown up, and, partially because of the position of the painting high on the wall, holy. It was a secret, yet also a trick that filled me at once with longing and resentment. On the river a man and a woman in a blinding white dress glided in a boat that was maybe gray and maybe the subtlest of greens.

Somebody made this. If somebody made it, then *how* they made it could be figured out. I stared. The receptionist gave thanks in her heart for silence. While I stared, the doctor summoned me into the inner office to explain the operation. I wasn't interested in that. I wanted to talk about the painting.

In the consultation room, mother and father sat smiling. That in itself was an ambiguous sign. The doctor lifted me into a vast leather chair beside his desk, where he summarized what was to happen. The desk surface was a gleam of dark glass, and on a little stand upon the glass rested a plaster model of the heart. Though I couldn't read the label, I knew instantly it was the heart, and I was in love. It rendered the two-lobed pink frivolities of Valentine cards preposterous. It opened into chambers, some violet-blue, some scarlet, criss-crossed with slim paths of vessels of the same gaudy brilliance. To be told that I possessed the original of this treasure was almost unbearable, like being awakened from sleep with *Long Live the King!* sounding in your unsuspecting ears. I asked if I could put my fingers into the chambers, and he said I could. He called them auricles and ventricles. Never before were there words of such nobility.

While I boy-handled the colored plaster heart, the doctor explained the operation. It was a thoughtful gesture, but my interest was limited by the knowledge that adults would do what they wanted, even to me, and though they asked my opinion it wouldn't matter very much.

I said, "This isn't real."

The doctor said, "No, it's a model. Do you understand—"

"Yes. Mine looks just like this?"

"Yes," he said, guiding my finger to the pulmonic valve, where my trouble was. It was beautiful. Someone would touch my heart like that, my real heart in scarlet and purple, just as I touched the plaster model.

At that instant I first recognized that the painting in the waiting room and the plaster heart were the same—objects made to be like something in the world, but not exactly, and that the space between identity and similarity was the point of them. The doctor put my two hands together to show how big my heart was. The plaster heart was as big as my head. In the waiting room, the painting contained a river and trees and people and a boat, yet I could carry it away if they lifted it down to me.

Magic. You could change the world. Bigger, smaller, brighter, make it last. It was power hitherto unsuspected, and I desired it profoundly. I should say I desired *them* profoundly, perceiving that though painting and plaster model *did* the same thing, they didn't *want* the same thing. Plaster heart wished to convey information. Painting aimed to provoke an answer. Plaster heart presented; painting insinuated.

Children are Puritans, and the intention of the plaster heart seemed so much cleaner that I thought I'd made my choice. I would be a scientist. Like an inappropriate but pleasant marriage, I carried it through to the threshold of majority.

The choice reversed itself so gradually and over so much time that I didn't analyze the process until after it was accomplished. I'd chosen wrong, but with sensitivity to compelling currents in me and in the world. It would be a mistake to believe that the distinction lay in the subject matter, in the fact that one was "art" and the other "science." The distinction lay purely with me, that response should mean more than understanding. Impressionistic reproduction and plaster model of the heart both moved me. I am a poet rather than a scientist because my desire, before comprehension, before wisdom, was to move them in return.

It still shocks me to want some things more than I want to understand.

❦

I glean details for my side of an unnecessary ledger:

The first art—the cave paintings of Altimira, the Rhine Venuses, Gilgamesh—is perfect and eternal. Yesterday's science is quaint.

The mistakes of a great artist create unsuspected worlds. The mistakes of science are flushed down the drain, laughed from the textbooks.

Some fine artists—Flaubert, Schoenberg, Seurat—think like scientists. The greatest scientists think like artists. I nearly wept with delight upon hearing theoretical physicists who deal with subatomic matters presently unverifiable by experimentation evaluate propositions according to their beauty and elegance.

Is it beautiful? Then let us hope it's true. It's our best shot.

.   .   .

Beauty is truth. We know that, always have. Both art and science wander from this truth, though science more proudly and for greater stretches of time. Kepler was the last great scientist before Einstein to believe that beauty would be the principle of truth in the cosmos. Art's apostasy has seldom lasted more than a generation.

Among scientists and among artists are those who reject moral responsibility. An artist who does so may be exquisite but is in eternity inconsequential. A scientist who does so is a mad enchanter, heroic, horrible.

The power of science must be limited by what science knows. The power of art increases with mystery.

When the power of science exceeds its understanding, the result is monsters: the hydrogen bomb, uncontrolled genetic engineering.

When the power of art exceeds its understanding, the result is masterpiece: *King Lear, The Garden of Earthly Delights.*

Scientists generally live longer than artists. This is a statistic. Most scientists are happier than most artists. This is a theory I have not confirmed but will stand by.

Artists capture the human imagination more firmly and permanently than scientists. Imagine a Broadway play about Lyell, a movie of Agassiz. Even exceptions, such as Einstein, are honored for the mystic in them rather than the scientist. This is because we love potential more than definition. In the words of Marianne Moore, "We'd rather have the iceberg than the ship, though it meant the end of travel."

I do what I do because I am greedy. I go to the forest to devour.

To choose art over science at last is to long for power so great and transfiguring as to be useless in everyday life, on the chance that, in some time remote or necessity undreamed of, it might redeem the world.

Redemption, you say. *Big talk.* Yes, I answer, but easy to do. Easy to begin. Point. Cry out. Remember this: The highest of created beings are the Seraphim. Their sole employment is to cry out, *Holy!*

Mockingbirds

Day came excessively blue. When I got out of my car I was singing. I hauled out my blue daypack and arranged its contents on the hood while I sang. (A friend says I remind him of a Chekov character because I'll sing for no apparent reason, without self-consciousness, as though I were alone.) I packed carrots, apples, home-baked bread thick with bran and honey and heavy grains, and, lest I give the impression of advanced granola-consciousness, two plastic bottles of warm soda.

The man in the next car had been sitting, waiting for who knows what. He seemed to take my activity as a signal to get out and rush up the trail while it retained its untrodden purity. I watched him for a while, partially because I came behind and would have had to make an effort not to, partially because a long-tailed hawk hovered over his head, moving when he moved, veering when he veered.

Beyond a bend where I couldn't see him, he left the road. I could see the hawk, though, and knew the man's whereabouts long after he thought he'd vanished into the folds of the Blue Ridge. I made up a story in which the man sought to spy on me through the trees. I told myself I'd be able to hear him in the undergrowth, and certainly detect him by the bird over his head.

Soon I too left the road to climb the Shut-In trail, stopping at the top of the ridge to eat carrots out of my pack, not from hunger but for the delight of the moment. I descended into Sleepy Gap to bask in the sun. Moments later, somehow behind me after all my detours, came the man from the parking lot. It was timed too well; perhaps he had been watching after all. He saw me looking up. He said, "I lost my hawk."

He was a fine-featured man, compact, with the close-cropped silver-black hair I've always thought of as elegant, and the pointed, delicate face of person who had been a fox in a former life. In his left ear lobe shone a golden wire. I noted that we were dressed identically, in Levi's and denim jackets faded to the color of pale sky, flannel shirts plaid in blue and black, opened mid-chest over gray T-shirts, white Reeboks on our feet. Both of us carried packs, his pale green and slung over his shoulder. It looked intentional, as though we were models posing for an outdoors magazine.

He began to talk, with the urgency of the Ancient Mariner, about ospreys, about hawks, about the trees dying on Mount Mitchell. When he mentioned Mitchell, invisible far to the north, he pointed toward Mount Pisgah, a blue eminence blocking the south-ern horizon, as though it were more important to get the form right than the direction. I wondered why this intensity of expression, why my sense that his subject matter wasn't really what was on his mind. Still, it was material I wanted to hear, so I stood with my back to the sun and listened.

Finally he mentioned the hawk. "It was right over my head," he said. "You saw it. Whenever I tried to go higher, it began to yell."

I ventured, "Maybe its nest—" but it was too early in the season, and we both knew it. We talked a while longer, he more agitated over the hawk than I thought he should have been. When at last he turned toward the parking lot, I called a final encouragement at his back.

"It was nothing. Just an accident."

That is one of the few sentences that I wish now I could take back.

Remember this: There are no accidents.

❦

From primeval forebears I acquire the notion that every encounter with inhuman agents is a portent. A butterfly brushing my
shoulder snaps my eyes open to what comes next. The track of a fox
beneath my window fills me with excitement, a vulpine Baptist
heralding a wild Incarnation. The twentieth-century part of me
scoffs at such speculations. The eternal portion keeps them and
ponders them in its heart, knowing portent before it knew skepticism
and determined to cherish it longer.

When I was five, my father built a garage. If you drove into the
garage at night, your headlights illuminated the back wall and the
wood beams where he stored tools. One night the headlights set
ablaze the lantern eyes and undulating body of a weasel, which
paused for a moment, baring his teeth in a snarl of defiance before
disappearing into the complexities of the ceiling. I'd awakened at just
that moment from a sound sleep in the back of the car. I opened my
eyes at the one angle that would have revealed the weasel among the
rafters. Nobody else saw it. When I told my father, he said it was a rat,
but I knew what it was, and I knew furthermore that it was a
profound import, a message from the Compeler of Weasels secret in
the starry dark. I didn't care that the message was unclear. Time
would reveal all. I never saw the weasel again, but likewise I never
entered the garage without believing that a pair of blood-colored
eyes was trained on me, drilling into my skull messages from the
Dark.

❦

I taught for a year at Hiram College in Ohio, my alma mater. It
was a good year, a fulfillment and a finish for many life currents, and
I knew that whatever came after would be so different from what had
been that no bridge would span the gap. A clean break, painful and
necessary.

Out of concern for space in the moving van, and because of the
feeling of drastic transition, I'd taken boxes of letters saved through

the years and thrown them in the dumpster behind my apartment building: old lovers, family, teachers, friends mingled with beer cans and onion peels. It was a grievous and desperate thing to do, but I've never regretted it—maybe because of what happened in the dead of night.

The U-haul was loaded, nonessentials sold or given away. I lay for the last time in my apartment, in a sleeping bag on the floor, not sleeping. Excitement or anxiety kept me tossing, until a disturbance in the back yard badgered me full to my feet. In the light of the parking-lot lamp I saw a family of raccoons rooting in the dumpster, bright eyes ablaze when they turned to the light, droll and grave by turns as they pawed the riches of the day. What they made of my letters I can't say, but it delighted me to think of them there, mingling with my life in so direct and physical a way. *Eat,* I said aloud, that a raccoon might carry my vestiges when I had gone.

Such messages are necessary because we are strangers and sojourners. Portents do not trouble the sleep of those who are home.

❦

What is surprising is that we should be surprised by anything. We have dwelt here a long time. A bland I've-seen-it-all expression fits our faces. Yet like wayfarers and pilgrims we go forth each day in a state of advanced astonishment. Like the stranded extraterrestrials some make us out to be, we gape and exclaim. David cries in the temple,

> Hear my prayer, O Lord, and give ear unto my cry; hold not thy
> peace at my tears: for I am a stranger with thee, and a sojourner,
> as all my fathers were.

Hot nights. The atmosphere glowers dense and close—not unpleasant, but as though one lived in a chasm with air heaped in sweet crushing layers above.

A pure heat, new: yesterday's torpor scoured by thunderstorms, colossal animal-shaped clouds rolling gold fire from the west.

Craggy Dome. I pretend to climb to escape the heat. If that had actually been my intent, it would have worked. I pull my jacket around my shoulders, savoring the exotic feeling of a summer chill.

If you come in winter you'll hear ravens cackling to themselves in midair, like sorcerers just that moment transformed, still carrying on old gossip in hard new voices. I come here when I am sad. Sheer spectacle takes the mind out of itself. That's why God gets away with answering our questions as He does, with whirlwinds or quasars or breaching leviathans. Our breath's taken away. We can't put the question a second time.

Mist whirls from the far valley and curls over the mountain like a veil before plunging down again, studded with fluttering swallows. It's a study in fluid dynamics, the cloud heavy yet pushed so furiously from behind that, though it clings to every confirmation of the ground, it keeps moving. Anything to keep moving.

The mountain stands before me, and I before the mountain. I say to its cloudy brow, "Free me and I'll come back to you," as though it were a god, as though all my contact with the human world were a calamity from which a prong of rock could free me.

When too many Winnebagos gather in the parking lot below, I climb down, scowling, a mountain sage uprooted by fumes and the gleam of pastel metal. Back into the city, sweating, knowing only what I knew before: There must be another way to live.

I lay reading in bed last night. I heard a sound of wind or rushing waters. I looked onto the hill to see if a pipe had burst or a tank truck sprung a leak, but all lay calm and still. I walked to the opposite window to see if there was a disturbance in the parking lot. As I watched, rain appeared at the top of the light and plunged with perceptible slowness to the ground. That was the cause, though the roaring preceded it by at least a minute, as though striking through the crowns of trees a thousand feet high.

A cardinal pipes hysterically in the willow outside my study window. I scan the ground for a cat or a fallen chick that might be disturbing her. Nothing. Perhaps the attack is from above. Perhaps she is scolding God.

Dream last night: grassy meadow at evening. Sun goes down, blooming of flowers that open under starlight. A figure in white. She shouts, *kallichoros!* I wake and find *kallichoros* in a Greek dictionary. It means "place of the beautiful dances."

Played the open-the-Bible-anywhere game. My eyes hit this passage: "Say not who shall ascend unto Heaven or shall descend into Hell: for lo, the Word is very nigh thee, in thy mouth and in thy heart." These things should terrify me more than they do.

❦

If they said to you, "Tell us the last time you remember believing everything would turn out right," you would think back to the summer of the mockingbirds, when bounty in the north or disturbance in the south sent them by the hundreds into Ohio farmlands where people thought themselves lucky before if one sang in a county. You would think of the locust trees, and the mockingbirds singing in them, the perfume and the whiteness and the music together. It made you change your notions about what is too little and what is enough.

You would remember evenings best. The farm women came out with pitchers of lemonade and kerchiefs to wipe their foreheads and sat on the front-porch swings, listening. Supper dishes would keep. The mockingbirds chased the cats all day, then perched in the lilac and sang until the stars came out. The farm women climbed to their rooms early, unwound their hair from scarves and pins, pewter and silver and crystally bakelite, their men watching them. That was the summer it didn't rain until the hay was in, didn't frost until the tomatoes were played out and the zinnias safe and scarlet on the sideboard. The black onyx Seth Thomas clock whose glass face always clouded in wet weather was fooled and stayed clear right to Thanksgiving.

That was the fire-scare summer, when the black dirt of Hartville burned like paper, and the wind was toward us and we stood by our fathers with hoes in hand to ditch our land safe at the first sign of burning. All that came was a golden cloud at sunset.

That was the summer Jack and I hiked down to the creek nearly every day. The creek issued from a storm sewer under Sullivan Street, where the houses ended, and vanished into a storm sewer under the B&O tracks, where the land was wild, the high grass exploding with the caw of cock pheasant. Between the Sullivan culvert and the railroad dicks, whom we never saw but who were rumored to bludgeon first and inquire later, the creek halved a ragged wood full of broken glass, and derelicts who slept it off away from cops and neighborhood dogs. We learned to catch crayfish and hang them on our shirts to terrify the girls. The crayfish bent their tails over their rumps of eggs and could live forever out of water, waving their claws from the dust balls under our beds.

That was the summer when cloudbursts washed shrews from their burrows in the hill. Jack and I picked tiny drowned bodies from the water, examined them carefully, believing them to be preliminary models, sketches in the flesh and not full animals. Their teeth were bared like stiff white thread.

That was the summer when mother took sick. The old folks always said, "took sick," as though it were something chosen, like bric-a-brac from a shelf. Once before, when I was very young, she had taken sick and stayed so long in the hospital that I didn't remember her, and the word *mother* took on an abstract resonance, like *Brazil* or *adolescence,* things heard of but remote.

They thought it would be easier if she left for the hospital while I was at school. When I got home, mother was gone. Instead, there stood Mrs. Dodd from church. Mrs. Dodd asked me if I would like milk and cookies. Never in my life had I had milk and cookies after school, the way they did on TV, and I burst into tears. I thought mother was dead. Then, ashamed to make Mrs. Dodd so miserable whatever the reason, I calmed down and ate her cookies.

I was too young to visit her hospital room, but sometimes father brought me to the street below, and she would wave from a window. What gave me a low opinion of the candor of adults I don't recall, but I believed then that she was gone, and that father had gotten a nurse to put on her pale robe and stand at the window to wave to me.

I dreamed of a figure in white satin, who spoke with her voice but moved like movie stars in the haze and violins that surrounded them in sentimental films when they kissed their children goodnight. Once when she came home I cried and pulled away, because I didn't know her.

People say you can get over anything. I doubt she got over that.

Just before school—I hadn't use for a calendar then, but you could tell by the new light at evening, slanted and golden—I came in from playing and found mother with her chair set solidly against the wall. I looked at her, carefully, thinking there was something I wanted to keep. She motioned me to her. She stood me between her knees so she could trim my hair for school. I heard the snipping close to my ears, felt her gathering the red hair in her hands so it wouldn't mess the floor. When she finished, she said my name, but I was afraid to turn and look at her. She was crying.

Mother recovered and lived productively for fifteen years, though ever after with an aura of fragility, as though she were the northernmost of some rare tropical bird, and each change of wind, each chill filled the heart with apprehension. When she sickened again, she was the only one not afraid.

She died at winter's end. I lived in the north then, and I walked to the bus station with sleet waving over the tops of my shoes. Laughing, arm-punching young men smoked in the back of the bus. The seat beside me was occupied by a stout babushka-ed immigrant lady who ate her single sandwich over 200 miles by poking into the bag with two gnarled fingers and removing, like an avocet probing under a rock, the smallest possible fragments.

I wanted to say to them, "My mother has died. I am going home now." Somehow I thought the drama would beautify us all. Through the bus windows I watched flocks of birds over white wastes, traveling north hopefully before the ice resigned.

I spent much of that spring hiking, always on weekends and sometimes on days I could spare—or at least *did* spare—from writing my dissertation. I preferred to go alone. Some days details of the world stood in memory like figures lasered in diamond. I could describe the cosmos compacted into the wing of the nuthatch. From some days remained no memory at all. I went out, came home, thawed my feet against the pounding steam register.

It's not that those days were wasted, but that the significant journey was interior, forgotten until the next such journey should reveal the secret landmarks and trails laboriously blazed.

Clouds hung motionless that day over the north, like a roof half finished. I drove south, where light lay blue and white like a dappled cat. I climbed in Pratt's Falls gorge.

It was cold at the bottom, still deep winter there out of the sun, but pleasant after the sweaty scramble down. I'd taken a feeder-creek bed most of the way, wading in high green boots, breaking the ice sometimes, sometimes walking cautiously upon it down the little water to the big one, the river shooting over Pratt's Falls. In a pool of the feeder-creek I stepped on the body of a frog. Woke too soon, maybe, or dug from his sleep by thawing water.

At the bottom I leaned on the snow that made an abrupt shelf on the rocky shingle of the stream. I wanted to sleep there, to say I had slept in snow, but it was too cold. So I began to draw in a brown plain-page book I kept in my knapsack. I drew tiny trees of lichens I saw on a well-sunned log, like miniature cacti or foliage in a book of dinosaurs. I drew liverworts that gemmed the same log like cabbages in a field. Behind them, tiny black and red spiders that didn't notice even when I bent in close. I was a mountain, a god, blocking their sun.

I'd seen Cooper's hawks over the near gray hills, and I tried to draw them, but I hadn't seen them close enough and realized I was drawing my memory of their picture in the Golden Press Bird Guide. Had I seen them only once I might have mistaken them for herons, flapping unhawklike on their silvery wings.

I could draw with my gloves on. They were my spring gloves and not too bulky, and my drawing did not require great delicacy of line. I finished with what lived on the log and began looking for something else. Wrens fussed by the water, tails up, screaming sometimes against only me, sometimes in contempt for all other creatures of the world. I tried to concentrate on them, but my eyes were drawn always from bird and stick into the stream itself, from the particular and sketchable into numinous water. I shifted from looking to seeing without noticing. Drowsy, I realized I had been staring for a long time.

I brought myself suddenly to, and when I did, the thing I had been staring at shook into focus. It was a dead doe, caught in a tangle of wood in the stream. Perhaps she had fallen from the falls or had been swept from the forest in a flash flood. Shot, maybe, on the bank and slid in. She was so thoroughly involved in the debris I couldn't tell where her legs were. Everything underwater was stripped clean of hair until it shone smooth and ghostly, like an unborn doe in her mother's belly. Her back was lifted above the current by the snag and was still furry. Her body was grotesquely contorted, elongated in the direction of the stream. She was not horrible bobbing there, but startling. I got up to kick the snag a few times, but it did not release her. Spring rains were coming, I decided, and would wash her down.

I walked on and found a path leading up. I didn't turn around, didn't think again of the deer. But that night when I dreamed, I kicked the snag away and she broke free, swimming first, then bounding into the forest. It was so bare I could see her running a long time.

That was the summer I could lie on my belly under the osier bush, reading, hour after hour, drowsy with the sun that seemed never to move, and the mockingbird came to sing over my shoulder, rocking the branch when he landed, and I thought that meant I would be lucky.

First Sight

C onsider the proposition that certain people see things other people don't because those things desire to be seen by them.

I hike with my friend Holly in Cat Gap in the Smokies. I poke under logs for orange tiger salamanders, bright and cold enough to be molded out of vinyl. It's early spring, and every watery depression boils over with toad eggs. They're appalling to the touch, like some blob out of a horror movie, and of course we cannot stop ourselves from touching. At the end of the day I tally up our finds, triumphant. I also realize that I haven't the faintest idea where we are. Wherever we look stands another version of one identical mountain, dome-shaped, cut as abruptly by Jurassic rivers as a baker cuts a mound of dough. As I dither, Holly points us in the right direction, triangulating by the mountains and the toad eggs and the rings of Saturn for all I can tell, and calmly leads us home.

A literary friend and I walk a whole day in the Ohio woods. By main force we keep the topic of conversation away from books.
"Well, what did you see?" he asks at the end, fumbling for the car keys.

"I saw white pine, wild geranium, raccoon sign, mayapple past its prime, beech, sassafrass—" I cease enumeration, catching a look of flat astonishment on his face.

"Well," I ask, "what did *you* see?"

"I saw greenish light under fallen leaves, how the radiance turned from red to blue as the day went, purple now, the undersides of things white in contrast—"

You get the point. Same woods. Same day. Same organs of sight. Utter division—or complementarity—of perception. We flatter ourselves when we put these differences down wholly to variations in human personality. Some of the credit goes to the will of the things that are seen. Does this sound mystical? Perhaps, but also plausible, even if presently unprovable. Anyone who studies life knows that no survival strategy is too elaborate, too encompassing, too unlikely not to have been tried.

You are an orchid. Your generations depend on your being noticed by a certain wasp that passes over your grotto once a year. They depend equally on avoiding the notice of a throng of orchid-munchers.

You are a gray whale. In the sea overhead fare two basic varieties of human, those who would destroy you for the riches of your body and those who would preserve you for nearly the same reason.

You are an April wake-robin. If your flower is picked you will die. If your flower is picked before pollenization, the infinity of your generations dies along with you.

You are a wild river. Plans for the dam are drawn, the access roads already bulldozed clear. The last scientist makes his visit. From your depths you push forward a little fish, unnoticed since the beginning of the world, alive in one green pool alone.

You are a biosphere, profoundly complex, profoundly delicate. Entering your west is an engineer loaded down with charts and measuring instruments, his eyes agleam with condo complexes yet to be. Entering your east is an artist carrying an easel over his shoulder. To whom do you show barren incommodiousness, to whom riches and bounty and mystery? Remember, a poem, a photograph, a passionate testimony could save your myriads.

Remember, their inability to believe you possess any such will, any such desire, is your final weapon.

.   .   .

Dorothy Wordsworth—the seeress of Romanticism, the patron saint of naturalists, whether they record or merely look—writes in her *Alfoxden Journal* on January 23, 1798:

> Set forward to Stowey at half-past five. A violent storm in the wood; sheltered under the hollies. When we left home the moon immensely large, the sky scattered over with clouds. These soon closed in, contracting the dimensions of the moon without concealing her. The sound of the pattering shower, and the gusts of wind, very grand. Left the wood when nothing remained of the storm but the driving wind, and a few scattering drops of rain. Presently all clear, Venus first showing herself between the struggling clouds.... The hawthorn hedges, black and pointed, glittering with millions of diamond drops; the hollies shining with broader patches of light. The road to Holford glittered like another stream.... All the Heavens seemed in one perpetual motion when the rain ceased; the moon appearing, now half veiled, and now retiring behind heavy clouds, the stars still moving, the roads dirty.

Dorothy walked perpetually in the foreground of transcendent tableaux. Her brother William's poems, and those of their friend Samuel Taylor Coleridge, are set with her observations like gems in cold iron. In her journal observations, Dorothy invents Romanticism for the English mind, centering on the conviction that nature has a message for us if we but look, transfigures us if we but open and drink in. The best artist is blind beside her. Her words incise like diamonds cut from her rainy hawthornes. Why did she *see* so surpassingly and unforgettably? The plain answer is that she was profoundly alert, receptive to the point of madness.

The *true* answer is that she was chosen.

❦

Affinity with certain creatures is a gift, free, unrefusable, generally unprofitable, precious beyond platinum. My friend David Factor can take you into woods behind the college biology station in Hiram, Ohio, on a spring morning and show you fifteen species of warbler. You'll have difficulty crediting such abundance until you follow with your binoculars an imaginary line shot from the end of his finger into the underbrush, gradually and laboriously zeroing in on the tiny living whistle box he sensed yards away at the edge of the forest. Hiking with David in a space no larger than a suburban yard, on two spring mornings I saw half the warblers I am ever likely to see, including the elusive mourning warbler, which Audubon considered rare and of which its very discoverer saw but one. David claims to pull this trick by meticulous knowledge of the warblers' individual songs, a claim he makes plausible by imitating them to, as far as my ears are concerned, perfection.

I do not permit him pride in this accomplishment. Knowledge of warblers is a form of grace descended—as is the case with all forms of grace—through no virtue of the recipient.

As a birder I have my talents and my shortcomings. Bad eyes. Good ears. Impatient, but with a general understanding of where things are likely to be. Nevertheless, warblers remain excruciating. I've seen my share, but seldom on purpose. My first parula warbler smashed into my screen door in Ohio, lying dazed in my hand before coming to and flying off in a ruffle of lazuli indignation. A black-throated blue rode into a convenience store in North Carolina one Easter Sunday in the hands of a woman who had come to buy kerosene. It too had crashed into some architectural feature, and it too came around when she took it out and set it on the sidewalk. A migrating prairie warbler rested overnight in brush against my window when I lived in a converted chicken coop at the root of Mount Pisgah. Some I saw while I was jogging, they assuming no doubt I'm blinder than I am without my glasses, fluttering bold and hilarious in the foliage at my ears. A male Blackburnian perched in the branch of a spruce inches from my face, like an Egyptian god with the sun's disk for a head. A yellowthroat landed on my boot while I was following a covey of gadwalls. A chat exploded in a red oak ten feet from my face, looking the other way, insolently oblivious to my presence and the heat of my curiosity.

The Grace of Warblers comes but sporadically to me, though other sorts flow sufficiently to permit a conviction of salvation. That of herons and woodpeckers, for instance. If I go to the water I will see a heron. It's that simple. Great blue mostly, but also green, black-crowned night, the species changing like the stars as one goes south.

·   ·   ·

I turn from the Maddy's Pond path to piss, Ohio, May, when every endeavor is transfigured. Before my zipper is wholly down I see ten pairs of myrtle warblers (now called, rudely, yellow-rumped), two of bluebirds, and a green heron standing spread-footed as the Colossus on the near bank, orange legged and fish-scale luminous, a god come onto the scummy water.

I bought my last car because during the test drive I was trying to watch a great blue heron stalk and freeze at the edge of the river while the salesman reeled off the list of the car's virtues. "Yes," I kept saying, "yes, yes."

A vixen whelped in the rocks behind the pool at the townhouse complex where I live. Mornings, she brings her pups down to sun and watch the human activity around the pool. The vixen is red, the pups red at legs and tail, but with silver saddles across their narrow backs. Human mothers bring their children up to swim, then stop a long time to watch the foxes, holding their children's hands, trying to instill at once both courage and caution. There they are, mother fox and mother human with their babies, each broadcasting invisible signals, each by the attention of her flesh saying *Watch, and learn*.

When I lived in Exeter, New Hampshire, I'd walk evenings to a wharf at the head of the Squamscott to visit a great blue heron. He appeared there every night. If the wharf stood forlorn when I arrived, I'd wait for him to flap back from hunting and land under hunched shoulders, a spirit infinitely aged, profoundly droll.

All herons are comic. Not *comedians* like chickadees or crows, but comic. Like a *zaftig* dowager in a Marx Brothers farce, they sail on unaffected by the wake of hilarity they shed behind. This is a function of flawless personal gravity. Human sages and prophets are funny in the same way. You do not laugh at them, but *because* of them, because of the solemnity at once lovely and incongruous that flows from them into the world. On Plum Island, Massachusetts, I knew where to find a concentration of black-crowned night herons. They are the Cary Grants of birds, at once funny and breathtakingly handsome. They stand in shallow water feeling about in the mud with one claw, like a man fumbling for lunch in a sack while keeping his head up in the conversation.

Likewise, if I enter a woods of any size I will find a pileated woodpecker. Rather, it will find me. I hate saying "it," but I can't tell male from female among pileateds unless they're mating. This my friend Heather and I saw in Corkscrew Swamp in Florida, directly above our heads and with a vehemence that somehow went with the flaring scarlet crests. Several elderly female tourists stood with us on the boardwalk. They asked what we were looking at, and we could not but show them. They whooped, they chortled, they slapped their trail guides on their knees. They tottered forward on the boardwalk shaking and chuckling. Mention this when people ask what good the wild is.

In any event, experienced birders have seen their first pileated with me, amazed that one so haphazard should lure this wonder out of the wilderness. I tell them it is not my fault.

On Christmas Day I hiked from the Chestnut Cove Overlook on the Blue Ridge Parkway to Sleepy Gap and back, over hills by the bareness of winter open to all distances. Whenever I stopped, the branches quickened with nuthatches, chickadees, titmice, downy woodpeckers, and most hugely of all the great pileated woodpeckers, Yule birds in their red and black and vivid. There were at least three individuals, two seemingly a pair, one challenging them with hysterical Gatling-gun calls from the periphery of their territory, imperial war transpiring in the treetops. When I disturbed them, they dropped low so as not to appear in silhouette against the sky. They screamed and flapped. Had the heavens to themselves.

Most bird guides call the pileated silent and secretive. Perhaps it is a component of the descended Grace of Woodpeckers that I've never found it so. I locate it by sound, a sort of maniacal, mechanical scream loosed at occasionally quite close range. Woody Woodpecker, the cartoon personality, is probably meant to be a pileated wood-pecker. The flaming red crest is right, and in Woody's irritating laugh of derision we have at once a diminishment and a parody of the pileated's blood-chilling scream, with wolf-howl and loon-call, the essential voice of wilderness. The pileated's other sound is the noise of an ax. If you hear an ax falling in the woods with almost-but-not-quite-human force and regularity, and you scan the forest floor without seeing anybody, look up. Watch the chips fly.

Christmas Day on the mountain, each surface wore its ornament of lichen, green, blue, blue-green, pale, and yellow. The sky possessed the glowering luminosity that comes before storms in summer, though a drop of two degrees would have brought snow. High on the ridge a twisted giant oak was shot through by a straight sapling, and to complete the composition someone had hung a beer can on a long string about fifteen feet from the ground, comically endearing, oddly lovely and in place. Nature and art in a single glance.

Unsated, I hike again on the Second Day of Christmas, the Feast of Stephan, proto-martyr, from Beaverdam Gap to Bent Creek Gap. I mention these names not because I expect you to know where they are, but because I like the sound of them.

On Young Pisgah Mountain, the very top of the world until you hit Pisgah to the southwest, stands a foundation of cement block, aborted and tumble-down, littered with those ubiquitous signs of human life, plastic soda bottles, which shall outlast the mountain. The area round about is a trampled glade sprouting bramble and tawny winter grass. In the mortar of the block are written names, and the date 1933.

Something told me I would see deer, and it was right.

The first time I saw deer my sister and I were very young, when an old buck jumped from the roadside and totaled our family's station wagon, off to Grandma's house on the day before Thanksgiving. The power—or at least the inert mass—of the animal at that moment made a lasting impression, and I'm still surprised at how small a white-tail really is. Cow-size I remember in the glare of my father's headlights, the red of wildness reflected one last instant from his eyes.

The deer is an animal with which I have no rapport, no grace. I know you are meant to sit in some likely spot and wait for The Visitation, but life is short. So I crunch on through the undergrowth, and the herds scatter. I would starve were I an Indian or a pioneer. Yet I saw deer that day, and what is as significant, they saw me.

Easing down the northeast slope of Young Pisgah, I heard hoof-falls, saw the white flags of nervous does. They were not very afraid of me. They loped off like mediocre actors following their blocking, and I thought if I walked with increased caution from bare patch to bare patch I might see one nearer. And so it was. I heard her and stopped dead. She climbed from the sunny side, high over the Parkway, into a grove of laurel thirty feet away. She was small, gray and dark steel–color, moving like a too-young dancer, not skittish as I expected, merely cautious.

I sensed the moment when she saw me. Her white tail flew up, then down, unsure what I intended. Luck put me downwind. I didn't move. She looked, looked away, looked back. Staring straight at me, she stamped one forehoof as though trying to startle me into giving myself away. She did this several times, making her hoof pause in midair for a moment before bringing it down with a sharp, alarming sound. When she stamped, the expression in her eyes changed, from an unhurried alertness almost to cunning, almost saying aloud, *Now I have you*. But she didn't have me. After she'd stamped and flagged and settled a couple of times, she did an amazing thing. She walked toward me, deliberately, casually, hoof before hoof. I scarcely dared to breathe. When half the distance between us was gone, she turned, without any gesture of fear, walked back to her grove of laurel, defecated, pranced high and mighty back down her side of the mountain.

The trail makes a switchback, dropping directly beneath the lip over which I had frightened the other deer. When I passed beneath they were arrayed on the side of the mountain like pictures on a vast wall. I felt the descent of grace abundant.

I walked on to Bent Creek, returned twice as fast as I had come. I watched the sun set behind Laurel Mountain, descending Young Pisgah in a flood of twilight pastels which to tell of were to diminish—flamingo and peony, turquoise and cerulean and cobalt and bluebird, gray and silver and dove, all slashed by the royal velvet of the darkening trees. I touched nothing, no tree, not the rose-canes glowing their unnatural lavender, not a leaf, fearing they would not be there. The mountain at that moment was not of this world. I returned to the parking lot in darkness. My heron-sold car waited in a shadow of blue and silver. In the valley an owl called, unfurling its quiet wings.

❦

The pileated woodpecker materializing from thin air; the bobcat, startled, vanishing back into it; the red cedar hammered into bare rock; the arctic tern hurtling 12,000 miles from pole to pole; duckweed rising from wintering muck to bloom in the pastures of the light: These are deeds of a separate world. We have taken ourselves from that world, so they strike us necessarily as hieratic, symbolic, in any sure and certain sense inexplicable.

This is well. Imagine a world explained.

❦

One masterpiece of seventeenth-century prose is the *Complete Herbal* by Nicholas Culpepper. It is in every sense a scientific text, as things were understood in 1640, and carefully distinguishes between those things that are "known" and those merely purported by the ignorant and hopeful. Culpepper never spares technical vocabulary for the sake of a popular tone, and he harrumphingly assumes a high level of awareness in his audience, as when he speaks of the broom plant: "To spend time in writing a description hereof is altogether needless, it being so generally used by all the good housewives almost throughout the land to sweep their houses with." Good sense, good health, a modern perspective pervade all.

If you look up *goldenrod* in the *Herbal* you will find a usable description of the physical appearance of the plant, its habitat and blooming time, with the added benefit that Culpepper's botanic descriptions read like Marianne Moore poems.

After the description comes a section called *Government and Virtues*. Here we see into another century. Of goldenrod Culpepper writes:

Venus rules this herb. It is a balsamic vulneray herb, long famous against inward hurts and bruises.... Few things exceed it in the gravel, stones in the reins and kidneys, strangury, and where are

> small stones so situated as to cause heat and soreness.... It is a
> sovreign [*sic*] wound-herb, inferior to none, both for inward and
> outward use. It is good to stay the immoderate flux of women's
> courses, the bloody flux, ruptures, ulcers... and in lotions to wash
> the privy parts in venereal cases.

Yes, it's quaint, but we do Culpepper an injustice to assume he is a
fool. His science is as correct and modern as he could make it. It
adheres to his conception of reality with elegance and completeness.
Nothing is untidy, nothing is left over or cut against the grain.
Culpepper is not only a botanist and physician, but also (and almost
necessarily at the time) an astrologer, who *knew* by reason and
observation that the fate of men is tied to the great dance of the stars,
who read the signatures of the planets in the wayside herbs. This is
beautiful to him. It is not "superstition" any more than is, say, modern
theoretical physics. Less so, for Culpepper would claim that his
assertions stand up to experimental proof, whereas the physicist may
not. Culpepper is wrong, but his is neither inconsistent nor benighted.
To the "vulgar" unacquainted with astrology he writes,

> Kind souls, I am sorry it hath been your sad mishap to have been
> so long trained in such Egyptian darkness, even darkness which
> to your sorrow may be felt. The vulgar road of physic is not in my
> practice, and I am therefore the more unfit to give you advice.

What this Egyptian darkness might be I am not sure. Perhaps the
waving of chicken lips or praying before Romish idols, but I suspect it
to be an early outbreak of what we would call modern medicine, with
its mad disregard for homeopathy.

Culpepper was not only one of the last men of astrology (magic
died a long death; remember that Isaac Newton cast horoscopes and
tried to alchemize base metals) but also one of the first of science.
After enumerating the received properties of the ash tree, he adds:

> I can justly except against none of this, save only the first, *viz.*—
> that ash tree tops and leaves are good against the biting of
> serpents. I suppose this had its rise from Gerard or Pliny, both

which hold that there is such an antipathy between an adder and
an ash-tree, that is an adder be encompasssed around with ash-tree
leaves, she would sooner run through fire than through the leaves;
the contrary to which is the truth, as both my eyes are witness.

Imagine the experiment. But the important thing is that it must have
been an experiment. Culpepper knew the difference between vulgar
supposition and provable truth.

His own suppositions are not vulgar, but airy, beautiful,
coherent, incorrect. Why?

I suggest his quaint world was Reality then because that was
the world that was meant to be. Not ordained by God or fate, but by
the play of Nicholas Culpepper's imagination over the ditches of
Spitalfields. It is not a matter of perception, but of aesthetics. Former
men missed Natural Selection and the Big Bang not because of
ignorance but because of the beauty of the alternatives. How *beautiful*
that the mark of Venus should be graven on the goldenrod. How
beautiful that the stars hang in crystal spheres ply over ply above
Foundation Earth.

When do perceptions change and enlarge?

When the mind changes and enlarges the set of things that it
can call beautiful.

Kepler could not let loose of his Perfect Shapes until he saw the
beauty of the ellipse. The religious establishment could not (cannot,
I should say) embrace evolution until it perceived the superior
splendor of everlasting labor over instantaneous will. Progress is
made in science when someone—someone convincing, a Darwin, an
Einstein—finds the next step unavoidably seductive.

Advances in knowledge are advances in aesthetics.

Beauty propels the sciences. Always.

Learning is seduction. We know the secrets of the mountain and
the rainbow when we begin to desire them. We change cosmologies
the minute a lovelier one appears, one that we long for desperately
enough to invent elegant experiments to prove.

As it should. Beauty is truth; truth, beauty. Remember that
one?

.   .   .

Why do I see heron and woodpecker and orange salamander when I go into the forest? Because they are beautiful to me. Because I desire them; and love, far from being blind, wears hawk's eyes. Why do I desire them and find them beautiful? This is a harder question and requires a harder answer. I'll come out and say it: because they desire me and, in some way unavailable to human understanding, perhaps forever, find me beautiful.

❦

Gathering dust on my shelf are at least four books that argue different reasons for the extinction of the dinosaurs. I can present my theory in a sentence: They'd learned all they needed to know. The towers of the Olmecs, the sanctuaries of the Cretans begin their decline into dust when the priest steps back, eyes wide, whispering, "Yes, I see."

Grendel howls on the world's weird rim. When the hero destroys him, he destroys an elder world, beats a blood path forward to the new.

The Visitation at the wood's edge is always fatal. It cannot be predicted or declined. You open your arms. You pretend it is what you sought. Who expected a prince, a carpenter's son, a camel herder? Dispensation is the essential surprise. Grace Descended passes by one bent on his preconceptions. A new world debuts not from the prophecies but in the mating of red birds on a branch, a doe striking her forefoot on the ground, twisted shadow of herons passing over the moon, a pattern hitherto unsuspected, a beauty so unprepared-for it must either be rejected or convulse the soul.

Traveling Companion

Who first looked up? That it was not a human is certain. Triceratops was capable of seeing stars. But did it *look at* them? If so, what did it think? Surely in some dim and vague way it thought something. Did it sow the night with twinkling outposts of Triceratopsitude, flowing with forage, free of prowling tyrannosaurs, where the potential buried under those knobby armories of bones might flower. What of Ramapithecus, lying on his back, chewing a stalk of grass in the Great Rift Valley, gazing through clear air into the Void? What of a Neanderthal, who buried her dead with such tenderness we know she already conceived for herself a soul?

The first time someone showed me the moons of Jupiter and the rings of Saturn in a backyard scope, I fell back in disbelief, as did Galileo's countrymen when he showed them the imperfect visage of the moon. To *hear of* a prodigy allows for a continuation of skepticism; the thing asserted but unproved need not be integrated into the mind. To see with your own eyes, however, necessitates one of two violent activities: violent rejection or violent reorganization of all you believed.

· · ·

Back in college I saw an instructional movie make the point that the same level of magnification that would reveal a hydrogen atom in my hand would, inverted, make visible quasars on the rim of the known universe. I lie in the back yard with a book on my face and a cold beer at my elbow, unconsciously the pivot of two echoing chasms, the unthinkably small, the unnecessarily immense. What does this require of me?

If you've ever seen starlight in still water you recognize that earthly life and the heavens have *something* to do with each other, even if that something's stretched tenuously along the thread of an unwinding photon. Remember the Martian rock I mentioned earlier? Scientists figure it's Martian because it's made of lava. Now, to have lava you must have a volcano, and to have a volcano you must be a world of some size. This lava congealed far too recently—about 10 million years ago—to be from the moon or any other celestial body we know of nearby. The best guess is that a gigantic collision pulverized part of the Martian surface and sent bits of it hurtling toward Earth. This is the most extreme intimacy imaginable. The queer red chunk I found on the mountain and put into the tank for my fish to swim around may have fallen from the sky, launched from another world in its hour of agony.

In his book *Red Giants and White Dwarfs*, Robert Jastrow, director of the Goddard Institute for Space Studies, plays out a chain of immensity analogies: If the Astrodome were an atom, the nucleus, the actual solid matter of it, would be a Ping-Pong ball in the center; the relation of the sun to the orbit of Pluto preserves roughly the same proportion; if all the stars in the Milky Way were oranges, the galaxy would still have a diameter of 20 million miles. Such information is valuable on its own. It instills a sense of proportion. Like the white sails of European vessels appearing as though by the power of gods in a Polynesian harbor, it brings the message that we are not alone, that in the grand scheme of things we are incapable of doing very much harm after all.

❧

I love antique astronomical chronicles for their sweet faith in the providence of creation, for their emphasis on a uniformity and invariability that is in actuality nowhere to be found. I'd keep the news from Newton, but it turns out that the steady firmament brims with eccentrics. Our own homely sun wobbles and roars and breaks out like an adolescent and hurls fiery prominences a hundred times the size of Earth toward us. Beyond the solar system lie cepheid variables, yellow supergiants that vary at a uniform individual rate, altering their brightness by as little as 10 or as much as 700 percent. There are the Mira variables, which shed luminous matter around themselves as a burning veil, then draw it back in a closed system of ejection and absorption. Some astronomers assert that all interstellar dust at one time passed through the crucible of a red Mira variable. The name comes from the star Omicron Ceti, nicknamed Mira, "the wonderful." This process would be wonderful enough, but there's also the matter of size. Most Mira variables are gigantic. Mira herself in the position of our sun would extend beyond the orbit of Mars.

Not to mention the cataclysmic variables, the novae. Once every human generation or so a giant explodes in our star system. Once every two or three centuries one explodes close enough to be seen by the naked eye at high noon. During its brief glory, the nova outshines a thousand million ordinary stars and radiates as much energy as our sun has burned in the last half billion years. What remains where the nova was is a neutron star with a core so dense that a cubic centimeter of it weighs a billion tons. If the neutron core is very, very large, approaching three solar masses, the collapse of the nova-remnant continues until it forms a black hole, absolute material zero—no, beyond that, material negative, a hole in the continuum. Theoretically there is no limit to the smallness of a black hole. A star with the mass of a thousand trillion trillion tons can shrink *theoretically* to the size of a jelly bean, a dime, a microbe. Matter in infinite nearness. How many black holes can dance on the head of a pin? "But," as Jastrow points out, "intuition tells us that such an object cannot exist." Intuition, or blind terror, a sort of disgust that something so excessive, so far in violation of human proportion should be thinkable.

These are our natural companions. In the face of them whatever we shoot into space seems quaint and infinitesimal.

❦

From a terrestrial perspective, however, our mock suns and artificial moons are Promethean, are more than half divine.

Thomas Chalmers, a Scottish polymath, lived in Glasgow, where in the first decade of the nineteenth century he began two series of weekday lectures, one designed to help businessmen incorporate Christianity into their daily dealings, the other meant to reconcile science and religion. Reconciliation came from Chalmers chiefly in the form of repeated instances of human smallness in the face of the immensity of Creation, an observation of greater novelty then and therefore more able to bear the purple emphasis that characterizes the good man's prose. In 1817 Chalmers published "The Christian Revelation Viewed in Connexion with the Modern Astronomy," which contains the following prophecy:

> In all these greater arrangements of divine wisdom, we can see that God has done the same things [light, heat, seasons] for the accommodation of the planets that he has done for the earth which we inhabit. And shall we say, that the resemblance stops here, because we are not in a situation to observe it? Shall we say, that this scene of magnificence has been called into being merely for the amusement of a few astronomers? Shall we measure the counsels of heaven by the narrow impotence of the human faculties? or conceive that silence and solitude reign throughout the mighty empire of nature...and that not a worshipper of the Divinity is to be found through the wide extent of yon vast and immeasurable regions?

People always suspected that they and the stars had something to do with each other. Mostly it was a one-way relationship; the stars looked down, affecting or controlling human destiny without being affected in return. Early in the Enlightenment the possibilities for actual relationship were aborted by the assumption that stars were a stupendously extended litter of dead lights, mindless worlds uninhabited and without moral consequence, shavings of the worktable of the Clockmaker God.

Later, however, the true hugeness of things dawned on certain people who, like Chalmers—though it's hard to tell from his bouquets of unscientific prose—formed the vanguard of the learned communities of their time. If those are suns, why shouldn't they be surrounded by planets, and why shouldn't the planets, sprung as they were from the labor of the same Creator, be rife with livings things, yea, even celestial Hanoverians presiding over far-flung emperies?

In Chalmers' essay, late Enlightenment man considers the heavens. The homocentrism of the medieval world vanishes as morning mist. Here a nineteenth-century Carl Sagan speculates on the billions and billions of prayers lifted up from the devout hearts— or whatevers—of the cosmos. Though the style is precious, the sentiment is not.

Chalmers, for all his variegated optimism, does not foresee an occasion to meet and greet these scattered brethren. It is sufficient to perceive and praise. Yet, perceive we will:

> ...Who shall assign a limit to the discoveries of future ages? Who can prescribe to science her boundaries, or restrain the active and insatiable curiosity of man within the present circle of his acquirements? We may guess with plausibility what we cannot anticipate with confidence. The day may yet be coming when our instruments of observation shall be inconceivably more powerful. They may ascertain still more decisive points of resemblance....Perhaps some large city, the vast metropolis of a mighty empire, may expand into a visible spot by the powers of some future telescope...there is no end to this conjecture, and to the men of other times we leave the full assurance...that yon planetary orbs are so many worlds, that they teem with life, and that the mighty Being who presides in high authority over this scene of grandeur and astonishment, has there planted the worshippers of his glory.

I pray nightly for an opportunity to employ the phrase "Yon planetary orbs."

. . .

Go to contemporary physics to find the vocabulary of rapture standing so bare and unashamed. But the sentiment you find everywhere, from vanguard physicists to the longing housewives whose sagas of ravishment by extraterrestrials empurple the pages of supermarket tabloids.

Centuries before Chalmers—millennia before Chalmers—the stars were not merely bright sequins, but Blessed Intelligences singing to the glory of God, the nearest a homocentric society could come to peopling the night.

We know we are involved with the stars without knowing why. Consider the fact that we are made out of them, out of their deaths and convulsions in the deeps of time. The iron of our blood remembers. Carbon warbles of its first hour.

My guess is that Chalmers would not be so much astonished by actual space travel as he would think it a perilous and unnecessary confirmation of what the eye can see quite well, and the heart knows already. Out there dwells The Magnificence. To some sensibilities, standing amid it adds nothing to sure if distant perception.

❦

I was born into the last generation that will never be able to think of space travel, if only to the moon, as routine. Some of our generation have gone into space, but mostly it will be our children hurling themselves into Chalmers' singing immensities. This is a shame, for it is also true that no succeeding generation will remember a time before, nor the arrival of the moment itself, at once millennial and prepared-for—like falling in love, not what you expected, but at once more frightening and more wonderful.

The night of the satellite was the first time events made a difference, the first time I recognized an involvement in what happened beyond the few back yards and playmates that were my universe, the first time anyone said, "You will remember this day forever," and I believed it.

I hung out then with a guy named Ronnie Roberts. He was two years older than I but had failed back into the same grade. I spent hours waiting for him to get out of summer reading class so we could be about our business. I'm trying to remember if I liked Ronnie. I don't know if I liked anyone. One's friend is one's friend, and, as in conditions of barbarism and chivalry, there were honor and loyalty between us even if nothing my present heart would call affection. He was important to me. Partially, this was because he dismayed my parents, an excellent quality in a boyhood friend. Partially this was because he was rough-hewn and outdoorsy and oblivious to the sorts of distinctions with which I burdened my days as a child. He had no ponderable imagination, which made him a perfect playground for mine. Perhaps it's enough to say that he was the first friend I had to whom I was utterly unsuited, so much so that we had to learn each other before we could communicate at all. The value of such forced accommodations cannot be overestimated.

We were friends for maybe two years. When our relationship ended, it had less to do with us than with revolution in the external world, an upheaval that changed alliances among boys and made adults reconsider the course of their lives. One could look up the exact day, but the excitement in the air was like that of the first day of school, or maybe just after when the newness remains sharp, the possibilities infinite.

We'd hiked all that day. Ronnie, uncharacteristically clever, told me two jokes I still remember. This surprised me, for I'd always been the joke teller. I liked Ronnie *that* day, maybe because of the jokes, for the first time seeing him as more than a co-star in a personal adventure series.

Generally he earned my admiration for things like remembering to bring matches so we could burn debris at a favorite campsite, or for making a whistle of a blade of grass. We spent hours with one foot on either side of the little creek that passed the Robertses' house, overturning rocks to find the crayfish and nymphs beneath. We called this "fishing," though fish were the things we saw the least of. I was a naturalist and he a hunter, potentially a great team, even if the potential would not be realized.

Though we never quarreled, that was the day I first noticed us talking at cross purposes. I spoke of dinosaurs and space travel and of fishing, longing to be forever at the creek levering stones, curious, delighted, unchangeable, and unchangeably a child.

Ronnie's face had begun to scar with acne. He talked of forming a rock and roll band, suggesting The Youngbloods and The Whirlwinds as possible names. I didn't know enough about rock and roll bands to point out that he didn't play an instrument, and my elementary school violin would probably not do. I liked the "Whirlwinds" better, but I really didn't like the idea at all. I'd probably jinxed us by once using the word *friendship*. What irked me was that he had stopped listening. I had been the talker, he the listener. That day he talked, not stupidly either, and I stared into the shiver of dry leaves.

One thing I liked about the Roberts home is that there was never a schedule. Ronnie brought us home when he pleased, and when we arrived, there would be supper. Deep into dusk we sat at our scorched campsite, recognizing that we had little to say to each other. His hormones and my imagination raged, and there was no room even in our loose confederation for all of that. Still, neither hurried to leave the ashes.

A voice began shouting Ronnie's name. It was his father's, a voice I didn't remember hearing more than once or twice, and rare enough to Ronnie that he jumped and ran, I following with the urgency of someone not anxious to be left in a strange woods at nightfall. It was a strong voice coming from a great distance, and we were afraid.

When we ran into the road I saw my father's car in the driveway, my mother standing beside it with my sister in her arms. It should have been a reassuring sight, but something in the strangeness of it, the unexpectedness, put me off. I looked hard at the faces as I ran, trying to read if I was in trouble or there had been a catastrophe. Everyone was smiling. Even that was not reassuring, for we'd already seen smiles that did not express pleasure.

Mother said, "We came early. To take you home. We wanted to see it together."

It sounded like she meant my sister, but I had already seen her. I said, "What?"

Mother looked into the air, unable to point with my sister in her arms. I looked where she looked. There, moving perceptibly, like a shooting star of miraculous durability, was a fire in the sky. Red, I remember it, though I remember the whole sky that night as a spilled burgundy flecked with rubies.

"*Sputnik*," my father said, "the first space ship."

Ronnie said, "Traveling Companion. It means Traveling Companion." He said this without looking up. He was already feeding the cats, whom he called with a long melisma made of their names— "Here, Scoots-a-Boots-a-Tang-a-Blackie." I asked if he didn't want to see it, but he went on feeding the cats with his meticulous single-mindedness, refusing to look. This was the sort of thing he did when he didn't want to do what I wanted but had no better suggestion of his own. It made me angry. I turned away, vowing never to speak unless spoken to first.

Mrs. Roberts had my gear ready to go home. I felt there was something more to it all than *Sputnik*, but no one mentioned anything else. In the car my mother sat with her head sticking through the window so she could watch the red fire sinking in the trees.

She said, "You'll remember this day always."

Rolling Stone magazine's history of rock and roll, *Rock of Ages*, reports that news of the first Russian space shot reverberated to Australia and into the heart of that great proto-rocker Little Richard. On tour in Sydney, he heard the tidings, saw the fire in the sky, gave up Tutti Frutti and Miss Molly in favor of the Lord:

> That night Russia sent off that very first *Sputnik*. It looked as though the big ball of fire came directly over the stadium about two or three hundred feet above our heads. It shook my mind. It really shook my mind. I got up from the piano and said, "This is it. I am through. I am leaving show business to go back to God."

❦

Summer night. Low music from the dormitory windows. Perfumes rise when we move across grass. I'm attending a summer-school session—eerily like Chalmers'—on the integration of business and the humanities. Our final session ends triumphantly, and partying extends to midnight, everyone happy and happy with one another

Someone sets up a telescope on the wet lawn. When I finally understand where to look and how, I take my first glance.

The woman guiding my progress through the heavens says, with appropriate ceremony, "That is the ecliptic." I look, devouring, unable to get enough. It is not what I expected. Not dust and smudge, but levitating hearths, splendor, vacancy, magnetic seas enveloping worlds of ice, continents racing across gulfs of fire, crystal mountains ten miles high. Bottomless valleys. Deeps and immensities. I was in love, with the telescope, with the smell of crushed grass, with the woman whose hand rested on my shoulder as I looked. Before you accuse me of frivolity, let me point out that it is a usual theme of legends that one's heart goes to whoever brings the most precious gift. My friends have been generous to me, but that was a gift of Immensity and Fire. I remember it now. I remember the smell of grass crushed where we stood watching a thousand million years of creation.

I am not able to tell you the meaning of any of it. I am able, like one of those irritating Eastern sages, to wink and imply that that very incapacity of expression is the meaning of it all.

Waters Beneath

F irst the firmament overhead, then the waters beneath. First the
   visible majesty, then the hidden. It's the way the mind works,
beginning with apprehension of exterior vastness, discovering slowly
that the same vastness extends underfoot, even to the recesses of its
own body. As stars link each to each by the pull of gravity, every
water molecule on the planet coheres, woven in a matrix that extends
from the bottom of the ocean to the ceiling of the atmosphere to the
cells of your brain. A storm over the Pacific stirs your blood. What
you do to the puddle in the back yard you do to the world.

   I had a recurring dream, or rather an image at the end of dreams,
that gave me comfort. Last night that image returned after I'd
forgotten it for several years. The image is this: There is a landscape,
darkly luminous, as of evening through stained-glass windows. Sharp
cliffs taper to a lake. The lake is unfathomably deep and far brighter
than the landscape. In it swim gigantic fish, sharks, sturgeon,
sunfish, paddlefish, Devonian monsters, fierce and immense, gleaming with the colors of jewels. Sometimes in the dream I merely watch,

transfixed with delight. Sometimes I feed them, the surface of the lake bent over vast, gleaming backs hurrying to eat from my hand.

One night before a journey I sleep fitfully, and when finally asleep, I dream. In the dream I travel on a great ocean liner. The deck rolls empty but for me, the atmosphere turbulent with the aftermath of storm. I hear commotion to one side. I lean over the rail, peer into water where white whales sport in the turbulence. I've got McVitties crackers in my pocket, the ones with chocolate on one side, and I throw them to the whales one by one, and they eat them, and stay near the boat. When, almost inconceivably, I begin to have enough of whales and turn away, out of the sea comes another presence. It is a seal. Golden, like the sun rising. It begins to sing.

Holly and I visit the North Carolina Fish Hatchery in the shadow of Looking Glass Mountain. If you buy a quarter's worth of feed, the farm-bred rainbow trout will surface in their cement rivers and suffer you to run your hand down their backs and along their sides. A live trout in the water feels . . . well, it's not what I expected. Soft and hard at once, like wet silk stretched over iron. Phallic. Solid muscle, quick and greedy. A little boy runs over to us. I give him the rest of the feed and hold him so he can lean out over the water to touch the trout. His mother watches. She is uncomfortable, but she knows it must be done.

❦

Any creek, any puddle, I'd be there with spade and stick to change it. I built dams on the creek behind our house until I flooded the neighbors' yards. Even when admonished I couldn't stop but moved downstream, under the cover of the willows. If I wasn't damming and channeling, I broke away snags so the current ran free. Anything to move or still the water, make it feel me. At one time I thought this meant that I should be an engineer, but it wasn't that. The power I wanted was the power of transformation. The sea-change. I imagined gray fish grazing in the neighbors' gardens, eels at the engines of the power mowers, our rooftops floating like dead islands of pastel. These were not, for me, images of destruction, but of redemption. I knew there was music audible only under water.

In winter, my task was to smash ice. I found a boathook in the woods once and used it to hammer rifts over the creek. I waited for the sound of broken ice bumping downstream under the frozen shell. Evil civilizations throve under the frozen domes, and if I could open them to the light, they would perish. All would be well if all could be made to flow.

Even now, hiking, I draw inevitably to creekside. I wait until no one watches. I dip my walking stick, lever rocks, dredge dead leaves, open channels.

Of the four classical elements, mine is water. Not that which stands so much as that which flows. Heraclitian by nature, I peer into roadside ditches as other men peruse the stock reports in the morning paper, and for the same reasons.

❧

Saturday morning.

I visit the creek we patrolled as boys. The houses must have stood as close then, the shield-wall of overgrown lilac thrown shadow just as suburban. We didn't notice. I notice now out of an adult sense of testimony, that everything be noted, regardless of consequence. I park the car and walk from streetside, having lost the old way among thickets and through lots no longer vacant.

Beyond the street, all is as it had been: the right smells, the right weeds, the right frogs *yiking* in amphibian indignation, the call of the right birds in the branches. I remember which flat rocks to lift to find crayfish. I remember old times, the boyhood fear when to pick a crayfish out of the gravel was the triumph of will over caution. Others were watching; it had to be done. The old hunter's excitement quickens my fingers. I lift; they lurk, waving claws in mere curiosity, too secure even for indignation.

This surprises me inordinately. Finding a good thing unchanged makes me at first suspicious, then hysterical with gratitude.

It could have been a subdivision. It could have been a Kmart. For it not to be, probably now never to be, is a peculiar and particular grace.

❦

The tempo of recent times makes us forget that a thousand generations of our foreparents witnessed nothing new under the sun. The murdering blue wall of the glacier. Carrion birds thronged at the rim of the forest. The same sharp, downward chipping motion to flake the same stone scrapers to clean the hides of the same mammoths.

Naturally, I prefer things at the white rush I'm used to. When I was born there were no VCRs, no space vehicles, no Disneyland, no microwave ovens. Computers bulked the size of city blocks. I remember gas at sixteen cents a gallon, and my father's exclaiming over the dispatch of the new interstate highway system that got us to Pennsylvania in hours rather than days.

My first creek flows as and where it always did: from Alder Pond—a vestige of the Wisconsin Ice Sheet, filling and diminishing even in my memory—through culverts under the city streets, out again at the "deep end" at the mouth of the Sullivan Street culvert, blue and mysterious, arrowed with steel-backed fish, shrill with frogs.

Frogs are unusual inhabitants of quick, shallow creeks, a fact I came by late because my creek brimmed with them. They must have been washed, perhaps as tadpoles, out of Alder Pond, under the subdivisions, through the culvert, into the boy-haunted shallows. They prospered. Leopards as long as your foot let you get close, then leap six feet easily, stopping your heart in your chest. Bulls blast in the green pools, heavy as winter boots. You can catch them again and again. They are incautious with ease and plenty. Their skin is not just green, but bark-brown and muddy blue. You hold them until by their own weight they slide hind-feet first from your hands back to the water.

Encountering mythology in junior high, I thought of the creek, wondering where its god might dwell, under the rocks, dissolved equally in the waters, laid out in the deep end like a child hiding in plain sight. Perhaps he took the emerald skin of leopard frogs, swift and watchful on the dappled banks.

At the bottom of the creek rot splinters of the Japanese flotillas we launched in imitation of the movies, bombing them with stones from the banks.

At the bottom lie the bones of the kitten Jesse burned to death with sterno from his mother's chafing dish, which I hid under stone and water in what I thought of then as loyalty. He mocked me as I did it, recognizing, perhaps, the futility of hiding a deed that we have remembered now for a quarter century.

Somewhere at the bottom, footprints, fingerprints. Great-grandmother with her stone tool, scraping, scraping.

❧

The tadpole pond on the heights above the creek has been bulldozed away. Life was always tenuous at the rim of fields dedicated to a vague but spacious form of industry, scoured and stripped yearly by heavy machinery. The pond's existence may have been an accident of a stuck tire or an idle bite of a power shovel. I say beside the bulldozed hollow of dry air, "It doesn't matter." To me, anyhow, not having interviewed toad or volvox. A poet before an ecologist, I conjure a pond in air, with Romantics testifying to the superiority of the disembodied. I carry it where I go. Midwinter I make it sing with the rutting of toads.

One toad species inhabits these parts: roccoco blotched, debo-nair-ugly *Bufo americanus*, whose garden-befriending myriads seem not to have declined because of the loss of one shallow breeding-pool.

The unexpected beauty of their golden eyes led medieval men to believe that the Philosopher's Stone, the charm that turns lead to gold, lay cradled in the skulls of toads. Christopher Smart writes in his great, weird masterpiece *Jubilate Agno:*

> Let Tola bless with the Toad, which is the good creature of God,
> tho, his virtue is in the secret, and his mention is not made.

Well, I mention him. May we all do so little harm, so much good, bear our homeliness with such oblivious dignity.

Toads are certainly the gardener's ally, devouring slugs and wire-worms and every creeping thing that creeps. Their uniform ungainliness disguises a uniform beneficence, a clean state of affairs refreshing in a world full of feints and deceits.

Mary C. Dickerson, in her droll and priceless *Frog Book* of 1906, writes, "One-year-old toads are so tame and confiding that we involuntarily wish them good luck whenever they cross our path." They are and we do. Few nonmammalian animals look so young when they are young, so old when they are old. In the baby toad at the pond's edge we read limitless potential. In the gnarled veteran of many summers lolling plate-wide by the doorstep we read a surpassing wisdom. These views are anthropomorphic but not necessarily erroneous.

Were I to produce the history of the world as a gigantic animated beast fable, I would cast toads as both upstart scalawags and Himalayan sages.

Furthermore, they sing. Ours produce a sweet, wavering trill, easily mistaken for birdsong until you see the singer. The sound possesses an almost insensible bass undertone, as if the toad's inner being, or the bottom of the pond, or the planet itself, gave back ghostly resonation. You can approximate it if you hum very deeply and whistle at the same time. All North American Salientia—amphibians that lack tails when mature, *e.g.*, frogs and toads—sing. The songs are produced by their forcing air over vocal chords in the larynx. Unlike the grunting of fish and the clicking of molluscs, these are true voices—in fact, the Ur-voice upon which the nightingale and Kiri Te Kanawa are variations. The first voice lifted over the waters was amphibian.

ಌ

As I suggested earlier, every molecule of water on Earth is connected to every other molecule of water. It is an inextricable black web, a pervading fabric, a foundation sea. God's separation of the waters of creation is material fact. The biota of the soil comprises creatures of the water, inhabiting microscopic seas that coat each grain of dust. This is the second-most-astonishing fact I know. What you do to a pool of standing water you do to the world.

When I lived in Exeter, New Hampshire, I went to the Atlantic shore every day. Every day. What did I do there? I looked at the water. Sometimes I swam in the water, though to do so was a decision not made casually, so plainly was he a cold green god, so plainly did I, diving, lay my soul against a greater soul.

A woman in a bar once said I looked like a sea-creature. It was meant as a compliment and I took it as one. It was the beginning of a notable relationship.

I tell you how to stave off drowning. Dive down. Embrace it. The sea will spit you back, astonished.

❦

One of my earliest memories is this: My father and mother and I are out driving in one of those dreadnought roadsters left over from the '40s. Father stops the car and says, "Listen." The moon pours silver on still water. It is spring. I listen. The sound is tremendous, terrifying. Frogs in their millions trill in a shallow lake. Because of the moon and the night and the sound from the water, I assume we have crossed a border. I think this is a new world, previously unsuspected, that my parents have taken this moment to introduce me to—related to the old world, but darker, louder, more vivid. Panic and delight war inside me. Mother opens her door, and the sound rolls in like waves. I want to scream without knowing why. I crawl over mother's lap, jump from the seat. I run toward the silver of the water, screaming, but not in fear. I have made a choice.

The equinox approaches, and for several nights the frogs have sung in the estate ponds across Chunns Cove. Hyla, the spring peeper, will call from waters still rimmed with ice. For a million years they've been spring's first voice.

Grandmother squats under the glacier wall, chipping her stone scraper. She hears singing. Not a bird, not a man. She wraps her stinking furs around her, limps to the waters to look.

Toads, though they seek dampness under stones, in cellars, in the cool of forests, do not drink in the ordinary way. Necessary moisture is absorbed through the skin.

To absorb rather than devour seems to me a particular grace, akin to the immaculate consumption by plants of pure sunlight.

The habits of the toad are ethereal to compensate for the earthiness of his appearance. He destroys the ravagers, slugs, cutworms, crop-devouring caterpillars. He swallows with his eyes.

Gideon, marching against the Midianites, divides his host into those that bend over and lap water like dogs and those who bring the water to their mouths with their hands. The Lord does not command him according to those who sprawl in the shallows and absorb. This is to keep the toad at peace.

The field where the tadpole pond was lies dry and yellow. I'm sorry, if not devastated. I count my losses, rejoice that they are few, but do not altogether forgive.

Even deserted it's a holy place, a place still visited in dreams. My interest in wild preservation began here. So did my interest in myself as a moral being. It provided a first chance to *act* in the face of an intolerable event—a small event, droll to think of now, but atrocious enough to a small boy to make the point that action is possible against atrocity.

Why I remember it was Good Friday is unclear, but I do remember, and that my friend Jack and I had taken our school day off to fish in the creek.

"Fish" is a misleading term, meaning in this context to seive and harry the creek bed for nymphs, larvae, crustaceans, amphibians—everything, in fact, but fish, which were too fast and clung to the deeper pools.

We seldom kept what we caught. Part of this was to balance Jesse, who threw his catch on his garage roof to die and decay, to add to his smelly but impressive collection of skeletons. He had a dog, a cat, and what he claimed was an oppossum, though under that corruption it could have been anything.

Part of our abstinence was that we were merely genuinely curious. Find it, hold it in your hand, drop it back into the current.

We fished up the rocky bed to the deep end, then up the steep bank to the tadpole pond, where we found sudden horror.

Big boys, teenagers we didn't know, invaded our pond. It was spring, and tens of dozens of toads had come to mate and lay their ropes of eggs. The boys stood knee-deep in the green water, lifting up the mating pairs and whacking them skyward with baseball bats. Toads exploded in midair, paying out gut and semicircles of pale blood. Some boys threw toads onto the bank, where others shot them with air-guns jammed down their gullets or set them sailing with bats swung like golf clubs.

A toad in agony excretes a poisonous liquid from its head. If you are a dog with a toad in your mouth, it is quite convincing. Against air-guns and baseball bats, even hands, it has no effect whatever.

I remember two emotions. The first and oddly the more powerful was the conviction that it must be an illusion, that nothing at once so horrible and so pointless could really happen. The second was a sly anger aware that it had to deceive superior force. I told the boys that I wanted to kill some too, and when they seemed agreeable I ran up and pretended to pitch them over the hill into the trees. I might really have thrown one or two as a diversion, but others I nudged over the brow of the hill with my toe, out of the boys' line of sight.

I'd saved maybe twenty when the boys caught on. They came at me with the bats and air-guns, and though I wasn't afraid they'd use them on me, I knew the time for subtlety was over.

I yelled *"Now!"* at Jack, as though we'd had a plan worked out all along. He watched me while I rammed toads into my pockets, under my shirt, anywhere I could carry them. When there was no toad space left, I began to run. I couldn't understand why it was so important to the boys that they have every toad, but it was, and they ran after me. Under my shirt the toad lovers still locked thigh to thigh, rutting and chirring against my skin. Part of the energy of my escape was disgust at their carnality, an evil purity of obsession that respected neither my sacrifice nor their own safety.

Like Hippolytus running before Atalanta, I tossed toads to one side or the other as the boys closed in, hoping somehow to save the remnant. I heard the sound of small bodies squashing under boots behind.

The boys didn't catch me. They must have given up, for I was small and slow and could never have outrun them. I pulled seven toads from under my shirt and set them on the dry leaves of a thicket where they would be safe. They kept on rutting, though what they laid in that dryness was lost. I remember *seven*, a number held against a day of atonement

They caught Jack and killed his toads. They hit him in the belly hard enough to smash their backs without hurting him. He ran home wailing, his shirt wringing blood that I thought at first was his.

❧

I've had three or four recurring dreams, all of them beautiful, one of the tadpole pond. Despite Good Friday long ago, its return brings peace.

In the dream a forbidding wilderness engulfs the scraggly urban woods of my boyhood. Sometimes its central barrier is desert, more often swamp or steep hill, which I laboriously negotiate, longing to get beyond. Sometimes there's a green plain of vines that one swims through forever without finding the end. Though I know all these things are deadly, they are also beautiful, and I move through the wilderness with hushed solemnity. Finally, at twilight, I gain the circle of barren crags amid which lies The Pond. Though The Pond is that same tadpole nursery of long ago, no one would recognize it but me. It has sunk into the caldera of a mountain, radiant, holy, inaccessible. I lean over the crag to look. The body of the water lies immense and incalculably deep. It gleams profound cobalt blue, lit from beneath and within. Great fish ply the waters, sharks, rays, eels, sunfish, creatures of every shape and of colors of light through the glass of a cathedral, ruby and topaz, cerulean, burgundy, gold, orange, velvet black. All lie radiant and holy and still, the waters churning silently with their myriads of burning life.

At that moment I feel perfection—not attained, but yielded, a free gift, overwhelming. I hold off waking. I look, and look.

The Landfill

The first, often hardest revelation is that the world is not as we anticipated—not even, in the final analysis, always what we can endure. In acceptable creation the man eats and the creature is eaten, yet we know in fact that sometimes you eat the shark, sometimes the shark eats you. What follows may look at first like a tale of disappointment. It isn't meant to be. It's meant to be the story of changes in aesthetics. To declare that what we like is beautiful is not particularly remarkable. To turn heads, insist on the beauty—even the holiness—of what we abhor.

❧

In 1781 Sir William Herschel became the first man in recorded history to discover a planet, frigid Uranus. Six years later he added two moons to that unthinkable world, Titania and Oberon. His sister Caroline, an astronomer in her own right, discovered three nebulae and eight comets. His son, Sir John Herschel, found himself born therefore into a family versed in wonders. In 1833 he published *Treatise on Astronomy,* which warns against the misinterpretations and "vulgar errors" accruing from imperfect or habitual apprehension. He admonishes the apprentice scientist:

> He must loosen his hold on all crude and hastily adopted notions, and must strengthen himself...for the unprejudiced admission of any conclusion which shall appear to be supported by careful observation and logical argument, even if it should prove of a nature adverse to notions he may have previously formed for himself, or taken up, without examination, on the credit of others.... We must purge our sight before we can receive and contemplate as they are the lineaments of truth and nature.

I pore through libraries for passages such as this, evergreen hyssop and horsetail of intellectual cleansing. Herschel, like all visionaries, goes to the heavens for illustrations of his maxim. The initiate, he says, sees gigantic truth behind the reduced forms of mundane existence, as the mariner knows the frozen immensity under the blue crest of the iceberg:

> The planets, which appear only as stars somewhat brighter than the rest, are to him spacious, elaborate, and habitable worlds; several of them much greater and far more curiously furnished than the earth he inhabits...and the stars themselves...which to ordinary apprehension present only lucid sparks or brilliant atoms, are to him suns of various and transcendent glory—effulgent centres of life and light to myriads of unseen worlds.

Complete knowledge brings, inevitably, delight. This is a truth generally forgotten, because partial knowledge brings, generally, misery.

❦

A byproduct of love for good books is an affection—ranging from indulgence to horrible fascination—for certain bad books. The Jane Austen specialist goes to bed with a cup of hot chocolate and a bodice-ripper. The heart surgeon showers, switches on MTV, turns the sound off, digs into a gamey who-done-it. The rabbi hides *Lord of the Moon of Blue Dragons* under the tablecloth when the bar mitvah boy arrives for his lesson. My own favorites are sleazy bios of the rich, famous, and miserable. Conspicuously unhappy writers are okay, but movie stars and power-diving rock-and-rollers are better.

Nobody minds a good bad book. Being caught with one is forgivably and endearingly human. But one gets the creeps from a bad good book, one that meant well, one that overshoots its target out of the sheer will to righteousness, one that, like a Baptist preacher at a bachelor party, cannot say the right thing. Ever. And there is no bad book like a bad nature book.

Of course, there's also no *good* book like a good nature book. Peter Matthiessen, Stephen Jay Gould, Lewis Thomas, and David Attenborough stand out among a crop of new practitioners whom both poetry and science might claim reasonably for their own. Annie Dillard's majestic *Pilgrim at Tinker Creek* changes permanently the way people must write—and perhaps think—about nature, blasting away the boundary between science and philosophy with the laser of flawless prose.

Still, it's tempting to declare that nature is sweet and dear, and here is brother grizzly bear to prove it. It probably sells more books. It certainly renders the cosmos more immediately livable.

Hearing that I'd taken upon myself the task of nature writing, a friend sent me *Little Brothers of the Air* by one Olive Thorne Miller. Published in 1892, it comes with an endpaper listing other volumes available in the series. Famous names such as Thoreau and Burroughs and Agassiz appear alongside treasures now probably lost to the world: *Prose Pastorals* by Herbert M. Sylvester, *The Rescue of an Old Place* by Mary Caroline Robbins, and my personal favorite, *Poetic Interpretation of Nature* by Principal J. C. Shairp. I want to read that. I want to hold in my hand a poetic interpretation of nature as it was in 1892, the year of Tennyson's death.

❧

Daring a poetic interpretation of nature, I'd begin here:

Among fluorescent insects is a group, normally caterpillars, that glows because they have been infected by a glowing bacterium. What appears to be—and is, from an observer's perspective—rare beauty is fatal to its bearers. They are dying of a luminous disease.

I'd reveal that spiders and caterpillars, stung by certain wasps, remain alive and motionless for months, a flaccid paralysis preserving them unchanged in their first youth, until the young of their assailants wake to take them as their natal meal.

That is poetry.

❧

Either my friend was being funny or thought of *Little Brothers of the Air*, rightly, as a gift of admonition.

I have read *Little Brothers of the Air*. Likely I shall be the last person on Earth not heir to Olive Thorne Miller to do so. You know what I found. Quaint anecdotes about Dame Crow and Mrs. Kingbird. Baby Martin's first flight. Master Robin's adventure in the garden. Miller tells no material untruth. She seems to have done in that part of her life related in *Little Brothers of the Air* more good than harm. This granted, she nevertheless exemplifies misconceptions that haunt natural and scientific writing from those of Aristotle onward.

The first misconception is that nature has nothing to do with us. That it is picturesque, sweet, "out there," or that unlike the world of men it possesses no moral or spiritual consequence; that it belongs to us, preserved when convenient, set aside when not. It would be pretty to think so, feeding as it does so many of our racial vanities. Preachers, capitalists, philosophers, weekend diarists join in aggrandizing the race by diminishing creation into two divisions, one portentous, the other decorative, both contingent. Yes indeed, the prairie is pretty, but it cannot count much in discussions of the real world. It has neither soul nor value in the full sense of those words.

As for the second misconception, reverse the above: that nature duplicates us in miniature, reflects us, provides real confirmation of our self-image. Here the connection between humanity and creation is acknowledged, but it is aimed in the wrong direction, almost always to trivialize the beast and brutalize the man.

On one side the cosmos gets organized into Miss Robin and Grandfather Mountain that we may see ourselves at play in all the fields of the Lord. This in the lit crit business is known as pathetic fallacy. We in the mountain is Beatrix Potter. The mountain in us is Mohammed.

On the other side—exemplified by that most sentimental of men, the behaviorist—humankind is the extended nerve of the animal, which is itself a little automaton of self-preservation. We are as they, unconscious bids for immortality on the part of a pool of chemicals. If we see parental care in the wolf and in the human mother, instead of calling them both love we call them both a mindless blaze of hormones.

If we enlarge ourselves, the world exists as a sort of backdrop to the great drama of humanity. If we diminish ourselves, looking, as it were, through the wrong end of a telescope, we see creation equal to us, equally empty and automatic, a mathematical necessity precious to a certain sort of mind because quantifiable and without surprises.

Like Samuel Johnson on free will—"Sir, we *know* we have free will, and there's an end on't"—we recognize the falseness of these views without always having the energy to explain how. In our best moments we perceive that either the dandelion is a spiritual essence, or neither are we. Either the humpback whale possesses an absolute right to continuance, or neither do we. We agree to distinctions of degree, but not of substance.

We go healthily wary of science or art that does not challenge our conceptions; it is likely merely a confirmation of a convenient status quo. We go equally wary of art or science that deliberately and insistently reverses the apparent; it is likely a self-delighting show of willfulness, a two-year-old screaming *no* into the light.

When they mistake, the weekend metaphysician and the behaviorist make the same mistake: believing that creation conforms to human desire. Or that it would be good if it did.

So what is the truth of the world? I don't know what it is, but I know how to tell it: every detail, every nuance, from the Dance of the

Planktons to the Fountaining of Galaxies, sung as Gospel. The one mistake is to make it too small. The one presumption is to leave something out.

❦

I'm not sure I've ever seen what a purist would call "wilderness." Nor has anyone. After Heisenberg, we recognize that our prescence mitigates whatever was before. When I step into a virgin forest, it loses its virginity. The instant I part the veil, the secret is no longer secret. If we wish to preserve wilderness, we must determine never to enter it; we must stop like Moses on the brink, gaze into the green wall, forbearing to change it with our first footfall.

Or, we retool our definitions.

Pioneers setting foot in Ohio found primeval forest stretching literally unbroken from border to border. Sojourners went mad for sunlight, for a place to breathe in the encircling green. By the time I arrived, you couldn't walk two hours without hitting a plowed field or a highway.

Who loved the forest more, the pioneers or me?

At Walden Pond I dodged water skiers and children bobbing amid bright plastic inflatable flotation dinosaurs.

I visited Annie Dillard's Tinker Creek. I made my pilgrimage. It is a suburb. As it should have been.

The man bent double with hunger pangs in the desert loves bread more than the man at the banquet. I love the greenwood better than any Cro-Magnon, because I can imagine a world without it.

I do not believe we'll be able ever again to define nature as that which exists where man does not.

Any further commentary on the natural world will add the cockroach to the condor, to the redwood the ailanthus covering the wounds of Beirut.

.   .   .

It's not what I would have chosen. In my worst moments I would swathe the world in green even if it meant the end of humanity. But it is what is, and sometimes it is possible to rejoice.

A Sierra Club poster proclaims, "In Wildness Is the Preservation of the World." I think not. In wildness is the Eden of the world, its innocence, its perfection. Having lost both innocence and perfection, it requires a different saviour.

Remember: Paradise is a City in a Garden. Not the City, not the Garden.

❦

What they wanted in the quarry I was never sure. Limestone or gravel. One could believe that place, Mordor-like, existed for itself, purposeless and self-enclosed, enduring in order to be the desolation of the world, except that house-sized trucks hourly roared laden from the gate.

The pits were worked by Allied Chemical, sprawling like a vast crustacean, one claw in the valley, one claw ten miles north reddening the sky in Solvay. Though you knew men must inhabit the yellow cabs of the digging machines, you didn't see them. Perhaps it was distance, or the angle from where one stood at the edge of the landfill, down, terrace after bare gouged terrace to the river valley. But the impersonality of the operation allowed one to believe that there was no human motivation at all, that there the souls of machines worked out their energies roaring and digging restless under the pale sky, a sort of purgatory where steel and rubber approach, through gigantic labor, sentience.

It used to be that men told stories of wise animals, human under their pelts. Now we tell stories of machines that wake one day thinking and wanting, near-men within a buzz of micro chips. It is the same story.

Let me admit I loved the quarry.

I make my conservationist friends uneasy because of a romantic involvement with industrial wastelands. They see a mad, diminished urban Byron perched on the wheel of an earthmover, surveying sublime desolation. Sublime it is, and the more desolate, the more sublime. A contemporary working factory is a money machine. An empty factory or a street of burned-out warehouses is the ruins of Nineveh. Even Blake was able to find something intriguing in the dark Satanic mills when he considered their apocalyptic potential. His divinities thunder like forges, steam like crucibles.

My very first job was with Goodyear Tire in Akron, just as most of the industrial operations moved out. I was a mailboy, and when I did the factory route I could finish forty minutes faster than the time allotted. I used those minutes to wander in abandoned plants across Kelly Avenue, miles of them, airy, dusty, pigeon-colonized. There I saw foxes, raccoons, a dead opossum that implied live cousins in the rafters. Snakes as thick and dark as tires fattened on rats, mysterious slithering monsters that must have found their way to sanctuary through all the dangerous and snake-detesting city. Brass-knuckled ailanthus pounded between bricks, buckled skylights. Day filtered through chinks in ceilings and fissures between bricks with soft, buttery radiance, a living yellow sometimes like sky before storm, often—if one narrowed the eyes so only light was visible—like the pale diffusion of a forest in earliest spring. If I'm right in attributing beauty to desperation, then the empty factories possessed one loveliness denied to the flowering wood.

One breathed an air of danger. If you had found a way into the desolation, what else might have as well? For one who had grown up with Saturday matinee vampires and mummies, each dark staircase provided a fresh test of grit. Also, whatever one was doing for one's soul, wandering about in the plants *looked* like goofing off. Mailboys were salaried, and the union workers sought vigilantly to find us in some trespass.

Most of the mailboys goofed off in plain sight, near the lobby vending machines where one could get bars of white candy surrounding centers of whipped blond chocolate as subtle as air. They would be caught, reported, switched to a route that provided more constant scrutiny. Not me. Never caught. Never visible. I wandered among the creatures, hidden in the wild as surely as if I'd taken to the Amazon.

I did the factory route so well and merrily that they switched me to the fifth floor, where the president and the chairman of the board presided over their council of plutocrats. They called it a promotion.

❧

Between the Allied quarry and the houses of Syracuse lay Skytop Landfill, which I loved even better, as one loves colossal wrecks that manage nevertheless a wild and forlorn beauty. It lay within comfortable jogging range, and one ran there in all weather, except the bitterest cold, to see what treasures may have been dumped, what creature found a temporary home.

Landfill wildlife was diverse and surprising. Deer, raccoon, rat, opossum, weasel one expects. But to ponds gathered in wheelruts came mallards in spring, raising whole broods until new dumpings erased their homes—new dumpings that let new ruts that would be next year's wetlands. Pheasants exploded from cover in their coronary-inducing way when you blundered onto them. Herons stalked the roads, as brazen and heedless as tourists, poking into corners after frogs. In the farthest, oldest pond—one that may in fact have been natural—lived a family of muskrats. Overhead on summer evenings a kestrel soared and twittered, taking advantage, as I did, of the openness of the place, bare acres scattered with scrub, shining with glass and furniture and defunct appliances. Sandpipers and the occassional coot bobbed in filthy water. You jogged, alert to wonder what might fly up at your feet.

Killdeer were the indwelling spirit of Skytop Landfill. Spring came when the killdeer came crying plaintively from the dark of the March hills. They call wild and sad. If you follow one, she recedes, still crying with her broken heart. Nothing you can do will heal it. Nothing you can do will make it worse. You know it is partially a sham—no one is that sad that long—but you fall for it; it changes a squalid dump into an opera of inclemency and survival.

South of the landfill lay a fringe of damaged trees. South of them, the great gap of the quarries.

The quarries comprised two pits, one long ago abandoned and filled with emerald water. When whatever commodity they dug became profitable again, they opened a new hole, lower, more efficiently dug.

Perhaps I should substitute "daringly" for "efficiently." They pared each week closer to the old pit wall, until a green lake lay like soup in a porcelain bowl, enclosed by a curve of rock that I could stretch my body across. People wouldn't do that. Machines did it, having no conception of mortality. The damp cliff face should have told them. Leakage in a tangled rope of extruded water should have said *too close*.

One day it could take no more. The rim gave. Green water fell four days and nights. I saw it at night, like a black tilted tabletop, smooth and gleaming in starlight. Had anyone lived in the river valley, they had been washed away. As it was, the furnaces of the much-haggled-over municipal trash burner went out; the goliath chemical trucks had to detour through the city, where people sent up a great shout, supposing they had sprung up overnight with their dust and din. Expatriated mallards circled, flew on. The moon leaned over, looking for herself where the water had been.

Plants should have taken over the lake bottom much more quickly than they did. Mullein tried that spring. It found plenty of ooze, but little soil. Summer withered it. Charms of finches hunted the gap, found nothing, homed to the thistles of the rim. You could walk there with impunity. It lay too high for the machines in the working pit to see you, dry and bare. Fishbones jumbled between the rocks. Ninety feet of water would have stood over your head. The rusty gleam after rains would be lost tools pounded free of mud, cups, coins, wrecks of old cars that you never looked inside for fear there would be bones.

Cold hit early that fall. When hunting season opened, a roof had already formed over the smaller ponds, gray-white and as brittle as eggshell.

I walked the dry lake then. There were hunters, several, or a few firing with maniacal frequency. Red and yellow shell casings shone in the frosty grass. Surrounded by a mile diameter of open ground, I didn't fear being mistaken for a deer. But why I'd come at all I couldn't say. I had work to do. It was cold, gray, barren, and the gunshots had the sound of empty irritability.

I saw a shape come toward me, a raccoon, maybe frightened out of the woods by the gunfire. Surely this was the purpose, to receive the gift of a raccoon on an autumn morning. It broke through the ice on the puddles as it approached, a noisy and awkward thing for an animal to do. It dragged something. A shadow trailed it across the ground. It stumbled too close, and not wanting a confrontation, I moved to let it know. It stopped, wearily, turned away. Its backside and one hind leg had been sheared away by bullets. Its organs hung in the air, like jumbled flowers, beautiful and oddly bloodless. Death glazed its eyes. It kept moving.

The guns began again, farther off, by the road.

❦

I would mention that informed views of nature are uniformly bloody.

I would mention that to views surpassing information and aspiring to some sort of understanding, the blood becomes irrelevant.

I would mention that there is a bug on Java, *Ptilocerus,* which wears under its abdomen a clump of bright hairs that marks a gland which secretes a substance irresistible to ants. As the ants feed, they might gradually fathom that the secretion is a narcotic, and as the paralysis chills their limbs, their benefactor pierces their chitin and begins to suck them dry. Those who have seen it call *Ptilocerus* profoundly beautiful.

Crossings

The vernal equinox. It is at once the last day of winter and the first of spring. I've driven north up the Blue Ridge Parkway until the barrier at Craggy Garden. I get out of the car, fuss with my gear, put on an extra shirt, start walking. Beyond the barrier the Craggy Pinnacle Tunnel remains impassable. Two breast-shaped mounds of ice block the lanes. I run through, because of the cold, out the north entrance into a wall of light. It must have been as bright on the other side, but I didn't notice. I keep trotting, to get as deep into the light as I can. Blue, of course, though the word does not suffice. Living blue. Crystalline. I slow down, as though the light were a substance dragging at my clothes. Snow lies in ravines and on the north face of the mountains. Snow-colored clouds marble the horizon. I am walking in a sapphire whose few snowy imperfections intensify the universal blue.

Except for the prongs of the mountains, I walk atop everything. If I sailed off the road I'd hit nothing for 2,000 miles, 12,000 if I flew east. A raven flaps over the valley, beating fast for so large a bird, chattering to himself like a sorcerer rehearsing spells. I am walking in a sapphire, utterly alone.

This is a crowded world, and yet I am perfectly, imperially alone. Houses visible under the raven's wings in the valley might as well be the moon. I walk out two hours, nap half an hour on a sunny bank, walk back two hours. In all that time the blue remains as changeless as a jewel in a pharoah's forehead. In all that time there has not been one other person. A feast, an orgy of solitude, and I gobble it down, with an orgiast's greed, and shame.

When I return, three boys bellow at and jostle one another at the tunnel's mouth. They take turns climbing down to a scenic place and having their photo taken. I should ask if they want me to take a picture of them all at once, but instead I try to pass by unseen, feeling I've arrogated something that belonged as much to them.

All that sapphire. All that solitude.

That they never wanted it is immaterial.

❦

Long ago I acquired the habit of hiking alone.

On the mountain I'm a monster of shyness, backing like an animal from the sound of approaching humanity.

One on one with the wild: It's an obsession that comes to seem both shocking and inevitable, like a difficult love affair at once excluding the lover from the world and giving him a special place in it.

Another person on the trail distracts me. If I meet someone in the woods, I smile and say either "Hi" or "Hey," depending on how far south we are. But I consider turning back, knowing that the trail ahead contains none of the surprises available to the first soul passing. Like a Castilian husband, I treasure virginity. If the other person is *with* me, the distraction multiplies. I don't mean to imply an unpleasant distraction. Few experiences are not improved by sharing. Just different. More an encounter with the other soul than with the world. Fine.

But sometimes you leave before morning, tiptoeing in the dark, carrying your shoes to lace them on the doorstep, your companion sleeping, or maybe awake and knowing what you need today.

❦

I'm very small, and sensible of the need to keep to the path, as otherwise the undergrowth waves above my head as surely as the trees. A man walks just ahead. I think he's my father, though the picture is unclear, and when I asked he had no such memory. He speaks. I don't recognize the words, and for a while I think he's jabbering on in the unfathomable way adults have. Suddenly I realize he's naming the trees. Oak. Maple. Dogwood. I run close, to miss nothing, touching their peculiar flesh as he calls the words out. *Dogwood? Why that?* I wonder without asking. The man is very tall, and I see he walks toward a sunny space where the trees end. I follow. It does not occur to me that I have another choice. Yet I long to turn back, to see these things that have just been named for me when it is they and I alone.

Great lovers know what merely obsessive lovers do not understand. In the highest love there is communion, but never identity. A perfect union of lovers is the end of love. The soul is always singular.

❦

Mrs. Timberlake leads us through the great south field of the metropolitan park. She teaches kindergarten, and each day she draws a gaggle of neighborhood children to school in her wake. It's impossible for me to keep up. I try to run, but I slow after a few yards like a toy winding down. I don't know that I'm sick, so I believe that I lag farther and farther behind, in greater and greater discomfort, because I'm lazy or for some reason can't walk as well as the others. I decide I don't care, and I sit down. Grass leaps over my head, hiding me completely. Green, yellow, tawny, the blaze of sky above. I feel safe and enclosed. I tell myself they can pick me up on the way home. It's a ridiculous thought, and I begin to laugh. Just before Mrs. Timberlake's alarmed voice sings my name over the forest of grass, I focus on a stalk at eye level, where a praying mantis arranges herself for a better look at me, her saw-arms braced on grass as one leans against a fencepost to contemplate the two-headed calf.

Same field, two years later, in second grade. Our schedules no longer coincide with Mrs. Timberlake's, so we walk by ourselves.

We're supposed to keep to the sidewalk, but we cut across the meadow because it's quick, beautiful, and forbidden. Also dangerous. We see him coming a long way off, Steve Benjamin, the school bully, older than we, and twice our size. He too has told us not to walk the meadow, claiming it as personal property. He leaps from the wood's edge when he sees us, like a young ram defending his mountainside. We scan, but there's no adult to whose protection we can appeal. Steve is yards away, so my companion takes the main chance and begins to run. With the head start, he'll probably be safe. I know I can't run. I plod along, conserving my energy. Steve pulls up beside me, panting and red in the face. He says, "I told you not to."

I keep plodding.

He says, "I want you to go all the way back and stay on the street."

I keep plodding, with my eyes thrown to the side, to watch his every move. I see him raise his arm to hit me. I turn, neither fast nor slow, my own fists raised. Before he can recover from the shock, I've landed two blows in his stomach and one in his face. He holds his nose. Blood runs between his fingers. I turn back to my way, remembering I wanted only to be left alone. Then something odd happens. I think of the blood. I think of his stomach shrinking away from the blows of my fist. I whirl on my heels, run toward him, screaming. He turns, runs. I chase him until I'm out of breath, feeling an exhilaration unknown to me before.

Tall Kurt pauses over a cluster of ant hills in a sandy space beside the path. Sun's admitted into the forest by a fallen beech, but how the sand got here I don't know. Maybe the ants themselves hauled it up from the guts of the mountain. In dry country, the experienced fossil hunter checks anthills daily for stone teeth and exquisite bones of proto-mammals spat out by the labor of the colony. Kurt stands still, contemplating. Finally, with his toe he nicks the top of an anthill, sends a cascade of sand down the hole.

I say, "What are you doing?"

"History. I'm making history. I want them to remember today."

We kick in two of the dozen or so anthills, to give it the randomness of a real event. As we walk, we recite the chronicles by which the scribes of the Myrmidons memorialize our passing.

Mike Havens and I snowshoe the sheer cliffs of Clark Reservation, near Syracuse. He's been talking about Coleridge. I've been watching to my right, where the glacial cliffs tumble 400 feet into the plungepool, black and deep, unfrozen at the center though without detectable current. It's night and I'm frightened, never having walked farther than across a lawn on snowshoes before. Sweat freezes on my shirt, breath on my beard, so thick I have to pick it away to talk.

We come to a cliff. I've done this path a hundred times snowless, so I know the cliff is there, but somehow I believed it would vanish by the force of my willing it to. Michael says, "We have to climb."

"That's a lousy idea."

"Then we'll have to go back the way we came."

I think of the narrow rock path meandering the cliff, the star-filled freezing void above the water. I think of my propensity to tread on my own shoe and pitch sideways.

We climb. How we let it get dark I don't know. I'm cursing under my breath, blaspheming every fingerhold, every agonizing straddle around the shoes. Mike remains silent, his way of doing the same thing.

At the top, pouring sweat, breathless, we begin to run, legs spread like animals three times taller than we. We've said nothing to each other, never made a sign. Anything to put that cliff behind.

Nights later I dream of it, wake up sweating.

During college came the Year of the Female Hiking Companion. Three stand out.

Jane was good for long hauls over hills, through bogs, into the dangers of local farms with their dogs and wild-running, bad-tempered sows. Jane skipped class to hike with you and expected the same in return.

Toni wanted to hike—insisted on it—as a cure for a dramatic case of panphobia. I'm trying to think of something outside that she didn't fear. One was glad to be part of the therapy for a while, until—after the dozenth dog barked or pheasant exploded underfoot or other hiker appeared unanticipated on the trail and sent Toni screaming at prodigious pitch and duration, hands over her ears so she couldn't hear herself—one thought again of the pleasures of solitude.

Heather was best of the lot. She could make a pun out of the name of any woodland creature. Gaudy birds—kingfishers, green herons, sun-struck warblers—hid themselves until her binoculars were raised. She homed in on salamander rocks with a hunter's sureness. With her unhurried doe-gait, she was tireless, ever ready for the next rise. It's a comfort to me in this changeable world that once every year or so we get to hike together again, in more exotic settings, but with the same sense of limitless expectancy.

❧

A friend maintains that the one irreducible social, psychological, daily functional physiological difference between men and women is that men like to piss in the woods, prefer it even to the comforts of the modern bathroom, and women do not. I have considered this, and it seems sound.

First, let me say that hiking is, except under unusual circumstances, a single-sex activity. Women are better off hiking with women, men with men. This is almost entirely the fault of men, who get, for perfectly understandable evolutionary reasons, show-offy around women in the wild. We turn from doctors and cellists into bull bison, huffing and flaring our nostrils and hacking at innocent vegetation and losing the way because looking at the map is not a masculine activity. Nor is listening to someone who *has* looked at the map.

Women on the trail remain calm, uncomplaining, collected. This in itself can be a provocation to the male, who secretly longs for some calamity by which he can put his woodcraft and his courage on display. Women out for a hike are twentieth-century individuals who like Bach and fine wines and anticipate returning to them, nerves smoothed and palates cleaned by the mountain trail. They carry civilization with them. Men blank out the memory of anything Before, the car we came in, the polyresins swathing our bodies, the traffic sixty feet below on the Parkway. Our ears cock for the stirring of panthers, the tread of the enemy's moccasin on dry sticks. Listen to boys play army or space adventure and you'll know where exclusive imaginative involvement with the imperiling moment comes from.

I don't know what women think of this. I hope they find it endearing.

No matter how enlightened otherwise, we men secretly feel that the ease of our micturition is somehow a mark of superiority, if only in matters connected to that activity. For men hiking together this is not an issue, nor I imagine for women hiking together. But when men and women mix, a little voice at the back of his mind will wonder every mile or so, "When will she have to do it?" relishing the opportunity to stop, wait ostentatiously, heave great and patient sighs.

The same friend mentioned above—a woman—goes on to speculate that the relative ease of men in relieving themselves in the forest is proof that civilization was made by women.

I buy this too. The reason that the intelligent porpoise doesn't really *achieve* anything is that he's just too comfortable doing what comes naturally. I speculate that the human male was in the same condition, hunting with his buddies, pissing luxuriously, trailing home to brag about it all. Woman, on the other hand, was uncomfortable. Build her a room. Line it with tiles. Paint the tiles with leaping dolphins. Put in plumbing. Presto: civilization.

❧

I don't hike so much to cover ground or get away from it all as to look at things. This proves to be surprisingly idiosyncratic. I would have thought flat-out eyes-forward walking could be accomplished anywhere, yet I must be mistaken, for I drive hiking companions berserk with my endless stooping and poking and turning over stones. For this reason too I go alone.

But for a while I had a good hiking buddy.

Accepting a hiking buddy is as particular and personal an activity as choosing a career, or a lover. It informs you about yourself. It tells you what you need from someone when it will be you and he against the illimitable world. Sometimes it's enough that he'll carry his half of the gear, or that he has a special stove that weighs nothing and tans you at fifty paces.

TE was better than that. Of course he carried his half. He didn't mention it when I wadded the maps instead of rolling them with the Eleusian immaculateness affected by some outdoorsy types. He didn't exhaust one by telling of past adventures in the wildwood. Though accustomed to the outdoors, he was a virgin when it came to paying attention to it. I could say anything, and he'd let on it was news to him. TE endured calm and delightable; he let me do the talking when the subject was the wild, talked for me when the subject was the world we'd left behind. Whether writing these things about him is a gift or a violation, I don't know. Gift is what I mean.

I wrote about us in my journal:

Footsore from hiking the bare heights. Brought TE here for a nightcap—probably a bad idea, since our bellies were empty and our muscles worn out. Still, the moon hung bright, clusters of starfire like clouds over the mountain, Orion three tight diamonds beyond my fingertips. From the valley bottom the frog-chorus already began, that ecstatic sound, next to thunder the loveliest song of earth. I knew great peace in the moment before I unlocked the door and entered the house.

I said, meaning the frogs, "They are early."
TE answered, "They are always on time."

As I walked out of the laundry room this afternoon, through the trees came fluttering a sharp-shinned hawk, his striped tail dragging like a spear in the air behind. Light stood so bright around him, the forest radiant, still all the mountain a stage set and ready, and he the single dancer. As I watched I heard my inner voice turn it into narrative, to pass to TE sometime when we hear a hawk scream over the trees.

Rose at 6 o'clock to go birding. The best we saw were green heron, yellow-breasted vireo, myrtle warbler, thrasher, towhee.

The sky was raging sapphire. Necks sore from craning up into hundred-foot tulips. TE waits for a bird book to come out that features birds' rumps, as that's what you mostly see.

Frogs call in the darkness under a hand of white stars. I walk to the mailbox in the terrific dark of a cloudy mountain night. A creature stirs in the trees as I pass. My heart leaps when I hear it, hoping it is formidable, even dangerous, hoping it comes near me in the black. I hear the footsteps run, pause, then proceed calmly away, sure now I will not follow.

Ate at a despicable restaurant, drove the Parkway in blazing spring light. Day after day of this blue.

Because I'm driving and refuse to go farther without touching my toes to dirt, we stop along the roadside, penetrate a few hundred yards into the blossoming forest, never so deep that we can't hear the highway.

TE asks, "Why here?" and I glance around for a reason. "Ferns," I say. "Look at all the ferns." I lift the fronds to display the sori. The seeds of fern confer invisibility. I brush my finger along the frond's underside, touch it to my tongue. Still, there's my shadow on the ground. Another tale shot to hell.

We listen for birds. Woodpeckers, crows, too early for the full tide of warblers. I chatter the whole time, as though the forest creatures are my family and I'm introducing them, longing for him to think well of them.

I pull up a log, hoping to find a salamander. I do, a lovely green-gold one, the color of an old coin or an autumn leaf. I bear it to TE, holding it in my hand the way you must, half between crushing and escape. He shrinks back. I think he must believe it's a snake. I say, amazed at his hesitation, "It's a *salamander*."

"Doesn't it bite?"

I touch its nose with the tip of my little finger. "You see it doesn't."

I push it at him until he takes it in his hand, but he's uneasy. I say, "Okay," and take it back. "Didn't you ever play with salamanders when you were little?"

"No. Gators. Looks like a gator to me."

We have our little lecture on the difference between reptiles and amphibians. The whole time, the 'mander rests in my palm. How cold the little creature is, how small, its claws, though I feel them, exquisite to the point of invisibility. I don't understand how anything so small and cold can live.

Prionosuchus plummeri roamed the Brazilian river bottoms 230 million years ago. Thirty feet long, with the tapering needle jaws of a crocodile, it was the largest land animal and most formidable predator of the Permian age. Also, it was an amphibian, a proto-salamander. I cradle ghosts of those terrible genes in my hand with the two inches of cold wood creature, whose skull I could crush now with a breath. I hope TE sees the immensity of it, for it cannot be said.

Exhaustion like intoxication, dreamlike, license to indulge myself in cold drinks flavored with lime. Yesterday I came down with a debilitating, muscle-aching–sore-throat-and-headache flu. Walking was an effort. My voice dropped a sixth. Sickness is part of the exhaustion, but the larger part is TE and I having hiked the Joyce Kilmer Memorial Forest, where we saw the largest hemlock on the surface of the Earth. So the withered lady with the anemone in her buttonhole told us in the parking lot.

Drove through mountains darkened with storm and cloud, dazzled with escaping spears of light. The forest itself is lovely, though with a different feel. What? TE calls it "eerie," and that will do. Too alive, maybe: like finding yourself in a terrarium.

The air is so moist as to be visible, especially over the little rocketing streams. To breathe is to feel swathed and healed. The lungs pull at their own corners, trying to get bigger.

I don't remember richer forest: life upon life, life under life, golden fungus gnawed by black-and-gold beetles, snow-colored anemone backed by wood of lustrous absolute black, the red of shattered hemlock, the silver of mist, orange and pale of fungus, rust-backed toads, gigantic millipedes of elegant dust-rose and pewter, blood-red wake-robin. Over all, of course, green, green, green, green. Dazzling green. Electric green. Moss green. Mist-green. Hemlock silver-green. Gold-green of tulip poplars diffused from 200 feet over our heads. TE fits in, like a young trunk pushing up in the forest. He catches me looking at him and says, "What?"

I say, "Behind you" and leave him looking at the green drapery.

A Blackburnian warbler harvests the path at our feet. We stand like latter-day Moseses, awestruck by a Burning Bird. Bird takes his time. Finally, impatient, we brush past, he yielding the path barely long enough for the seams of our jeans to get by.

It rains. It leaves off raining. We are damp and as indifferent as the trees.

I regret being ill, for no forest has rung such a chord of *belonging*, as though I had dwelt there primevally and must return. If one lay down on the venereal soil one would before a week was out sprout ferns and fronds. One would harbor salamanders in the creases of one's clothes.

Stay a fortnight and transfigure to an animal.

Stay a month and be a god.

Deep crying of frogs in the night. Somewhere I picked up the notion that things must be mine before I can love them.

TE and I met for breakfast Friday. In some ways he is very young. He sings to himself when he rides, carrying on private dramas and dialogues—not oblivious to me but comfortable with me—in a way I do only when alone and perhaps not at all anymore.

He wanted a long ride, so we drove to Mount Mitchell. I don't know what his drama turned to, but I was Shelley balanced on the rim of Arve, the blasts and mists of Blanc raging around. A poet who knew his business could make this the axis of the world.

Mist ripped upward through the firs, meeting cloud in whirling air above the mountain. Ravens flew low in the mist, sorcerers in bird-shape, appearing and disappearing as they wove the thicknesses, their harsh voices like damaged voices of men.

We climbed the cement tower, left coins at all four corners for the gods of the mountain. Cold and beautiful. Clouds shifted over.

We ate in the little restaurant on the edge of the mountain, seeing nothing for the blank of the mist. We drove down again into Asheville, like prophets descended from the face of God.

TE listens. Nothing seems to be lost. He quotes what I have said. I think back, back, to an offhand comment weeks before that I had forgotten itself. It's a burden. I will have to say what I mean.

Pouring sweat as I write, as though it were a matter of honor not to turn on the air conditioner before morning. Sky a raging turquoise, punched at the top with stars.

When I returned, two huge dogs and a little toad were seated on my doorstep. I am trying to hammer them into images of grace.

TE says I hoard all these things for weapons, to wield them when the time is ripe. It sounds violent and calculating, but I suppose it's right.

Night heat. Chirring of cicadae. A mockingbird sang; I looked to see what disturbed him, but universal darkness took the mountain away. Perhaps he was singing out his dream.

I quote poetry at TE as we go. If it's funny, he laughs. If it's serious, he keeps silent, keeps walking. Whether this is awe or admonition I don't know. Maybe he senses that the words stand outside the things they mean, like a tree beside another tree. I want them to be the same thing—the word and the object it signals. I say so, He keeps walking.

TE says. "You're different in the woods." I accept that as a statement of fact, until I realize he's almost never known me elsewhere. He must be right, though; we all are.

If you hike alone you see the world. If you hike with an acquaintance you see him. If you hike with a friend you see yourself. You must decide what is necessary.

He won't hike in the snow, not that there's much around here anyway. I prepare to accuse him of being afraid, then realize I want to put myself into that danger and discomfort because I too am afraid. Old bravado. Handy sometimes, but not now.

I should remember, too, the odd shape of his stockinged feet, blunted on the left foot where he lost the second and third toes to frostbite. A spring rain soaking through whitens his face with pain.

Thank God, I say secretly, put down my boots, take up the cocoa tin.

❦

Holly and I hike in the shadow of Pisgah one morning late this winter. We come across the purple knit hat I know is TE's. I smell his smell on it, at once comforting and lonely, though whether the loneliness is his or mine I don't know. I should think first of danger, that he may be lost or hurt in the woods, but it doesn't seem very likely. It crosses my mind that he has foreseen we would pass this way and left us a memento.

Holly reads my mind. She says, "Somebody you know?"

Inexplicably, I answer, "No."

A mile or so farther along, I take my hat off, put his on. I give Holly my hat, and the circle stands complete.

Probes

C uriosity requires separateness. The act of scrutiny, however impassioned, implies that the scrutinizer stands *here,* the object *there*. We are so accustomed to this state that it seems remarkable only during bouts of morbid philosophizing. Yet, think of Adam, the creatures backing from him after that First Bad Day, he wondering initially *What are you doing?,* then, horribly, *What have I done?*

❦

Tourists were feeding the bears. They stayed in their cars, as the signs warned them to do, and the black bears, mostly females with young, politely waited for the food to be dropped on the ground. There were a few ruined paint jobs, maybe, but many would think that a small price to pay to be so near a wild animal.

The cubs bawled when they thought they weren't getting enough. Bread, Fritos, chips, Twinkies, pretzels, one idiot pouring beer in his hand, then letting it drip on an upturned muzzle.

I parked a way off, wanting to hike but not wanting to deal with either tourists or bears. I had a pack the colors of an American flag then, red, white, and blue in shiny material like vinyl but supple and warm to the touch, that my sister had bought for me during the Bicentennial. This story is partially to tell her what happened, as she never saw me use it. That day I used it, hoisting it on my back and scurrying into the woods in late spring, when anemones and bloodroots put forth their last efforts under the opening buds of the trees.

Fifty feet from the road I encountered the old bear sow. I saw no cub, but her teats looked swollen, and perhaps she'd cuffed it up a tree when she saw me coming. People in cars on the highway were one thing. Natural. A lone man in the forest was another. A threat, an invasion. Or perhaps an opportunity meant for her alone. Her posture said indecision. She shook her head slowly, an indication of anxiety that I figured she'd get over if I neither hesitated nor increased my pace. She'd see I was no threat. I meant to pass calmly on, turning neither right nor left. It was for this that I had mastered the ways of the forest.

I wasn't afraid even when she came close, even when she reared back on her hind legs in a gesture that may have been meant as a threat but that coming from her seemed comic and ungainly. I turned away, continued into the forest. She was quiet, and I didn't hear her moving over the leaf litter.

My neck snapped backward in a stationary whiplash when she bit into the American flag backpack, pushing my body violently forward with her paws to separate it from me. It worked. I felt the shoulderstraps rip, the sudden cool of air on my back. I knew enough not to run. I turned to watch, not afraid, not angry, merely astonished. I said out loud, in a tone of shocked betrayal that makes my remembrance smile, "Why are you doing this to me?"

A few rips told her that there was nothing edible in the backpack. She backed up a few paces in order to look at my face. She was curious. It didn't cross my mind that she would attack. Perhaps it didn't cross hers, either; bears are very powerful animals, even a runty black sow like mine, and she may have intended only an uninterested push to check my solidity. I stood as motionless as a stump, refusing to believe that I could be so without a clue as to what was happening, and why. I remember thinking nothing at all, not knowing where to start. Perhaps that's what saved me. When I did think again, I lay flat on my back, watching the bear's innocent behind disappear into the undergrowth. My patriotic backpack hung from her muzzle. My left pant leg was gone, and in my leg was a gash eight inches long where her claw had dug the flesh. I don't remember it, but I assume she stood to look me in the eye, then used my leg to steady herself coming down. She meant no harm. She was merely curious.

I came out of the forest that day with a cut leg and a sense of grievance. Not that the thing had happened, but that I did not see the point. Given the same occasion, I would sit, wait, watch, determined to know why.

❦

Rumors fly.

Voices whisper: The world may not be as we believed—it may be more beautiful, more dangerous, more fragile, more foreign. We resist, for to change world view is to change selves, and we're not ready. Denial is a great force, and we deny for years before the voices start again. Finally, someone suggests that truth is better than comfort. It sounds right. We try to agree. We burn old scriptures, march in the streets, turn against the teaching of our fathers. Still, we don't see it. We say, "How shall we come to know?"

Someone answers that we must put on new eyes. We must see the world as at the first, preconceptions cut away, and along with the preconceptions, safety. We must be children thrown from our former house, abandoned in the Greenwood, left to find the way by scattering crumbs behind us.

"It's too hard!" we say, turning back. But the house is already gone. Sparrows hop from foot to foot, waiting for the next crumb. The only way is forward.

This is called setting out. This is called the first step.

❦

I used to carry compact duodecimo notebooks with me when I hiked. Six or eight of them sit on my shelf, full of nonsequential notations about the forest or the state of my mind. Sketches, too, some of them quite good. (This surprises me, as I never think of myself as an artist. I killed that when I bought a camera.) I was young when I made those notations, and the sophomoric profundity of some of the passages is mortifying now. Still, I recognize what I was trying to do, and that I still do it, with a sense of reserve that is a function of literary style rather than any essential change of heart. If I wrote of or drew some wild creature in the book, I'd try to say its meaning, I'd try to distinguish from its ordinary functions some eternal message, a Platonic vibration that I would feel if I touched it deeply enough. I wanted essences, quiddities, believing that's what I was given a mind to find. I reeled out the names of things like litanies. I stained the pages with the sap of bloodroot and smears of dirt from flowering hills, to have the data with me at all times, to approach the critical mass. Information fermented among trail guides and spare socks. I wrote prayers in green ink, the entire burden of which seems to be *Let me see!*

Did I see? I don't know how to tell you. The answer is, of course, yes and no. I saw something. Not what I expected. Maybe the best answer is this:

I still carry a notebook into the forest, zippered into my backpack in the essentials partition along with knife and matches. The pages lie absolutely blank, as they have for several years. I carry the record book but do not record, like an agnostic who still packs his Bible for a journey.

The difference is that I have no doubt whatever.

❧

You are a Martian scientist. The temperature of your planet under extraordinary conditions approaches the thawing point of ice. Your thin, freezing atmosphere lets stars shine through at midday, except during stupendous red sandstorms that block the sky for weeks, guttering out at last against the flanks of volcanos ten miles high. Two tiny moons, dimmer than stars and as irregular as grains of dust, wander overhead. The world is dry, cold, violent, beautiful. From creation it has been this way. It is as worlds are.

Yet you hear queer reports. Inexplicable complexities of metal fall onto the desert. Those who find them claim they whirr and clank for a while before succumbing to the cold, like newborns lacking the sense to find shelter. One or two insist that they have fallen from the sky. You find that plausible if extreme. You aim your instruments. In all the blackness around your sun there is one candidate, one more conceivable Home.

You send to the third planet—the changeable blue world—a scientific probe equipped with sensors to detect what you conceive reality to be: hard, definite, palpable, brittle, cold, red, and sandy. Your expectations are low. You prepare for failure.

Your probe lands on the roof of a house. Roof registers fine, possessing several qualities you think of as real. You consider the data and record with unconcealed elation, "A roof!"

The probe bores through the roof into the room below. The room is full of perfumes, of Bach from the stereo, of the smells of cooking. But nothing hard, definite, sandy, so the sensors register zero and continue down. "An empty room," you write into the log, hope for quantifiable data dimming. Finally, with a clink audible to the astonished inhabitants of the room, the probe touches the cork of a bottle of Château Neuf du Papé, 1963, saved for just this evening in just this liquid season of the year. The cork is massy and palpable, and you cry to your recorder, "There's something here!" The probe punctures the cork, continues into the arterial red of the wine. But Martian reality does not allow for nose, bouquet, the slight stone savor of that sunny, exquisite year, and when you break through the bottom of the bottle you record, "Empty container."

Whoever was here has gone. A dead planet, torrid, watery, too dramatic for life as it is known. In its own way, perhaps, beautiful.

❦

You are God, and you have decided to make an oak. The problem is that each hillside, each damp river bottom demands a separate perfection. Yet you begin, and in a thousand generations you have made 300 different variations of a basic plan. Some shoot up like columns, braving the sky. Some cling to the tundra, bellying along like soldiers in a trench. Some bear sweet acorns that mature in a single season to fatten peccaries and black bears and marginal human communities and spread a shade of round-lobed foliage over the forest floor. Some bear bitter acorns that take two years to ripen, hurl a darkness over the ground like the points of spears.

Making an oak, you see that single vision does not suffice. You loosen the bonds, step back, let riot prevail. You divide yourself from the current. Bounty gathers on the planet. You choose as your form the whirlwind. No, it's not what they expected. Chaos, jostling in the wind. It's what they get.

❧

Sometimes, the point is not even what is *there*.

I hate this as much as you do. I'm telling you what I know, not what I like.

The Tao asserts that the significant part of the bowl is the empty space it encloses.

Consider. What's the story of the flower divorced from the heavy body of the bee, who visits, vanishes, secret as a god?

What are the odds against looking at precisely the right instant?

Without the bee, the blossom is an ornament, and there are no ornaments. It's all pointless without the Visitation, the Indwelling of emptiness.

Huston Smith recorded Tibetan monks at meditation singing chords at a bone-vibrating bass, *each* monk singing a chord, triads thundered from single throats. How is it done? Simply: You empty and purge until your being is a hollow vessel for the voice of God to blow into. Try it. To add to the self is relatively simple. A holy subtraction is the task of a lifetime.

Song, of course, is vacancy. A subtraction. A reverberation possible only where the body is not.

You are an earless race. You send your probe. In the hive, the nightingale's nest, the volcano's throat, you hear nothing.

What if the critical mass is reached, and it reveals that the essence is emptiness? What do you write in your notebook then? You wait, unwilling for that to be the answer. You take the high path under the beeches, waiting for the cosmos to stop joking.

At the beginning of September I bought tropical fish. My young friend Kevin Fakhoury sold me an expensive setup for $25, the remnant of an abandoned pet-shop business. I filled it with neon tetras and peacock-tail guppies in gold and purple, and four blue-gray ministering bottom cats. All are transparent, their guts, their hair-bones naked to the eye under vivid, taut tissue. When the water is clear they appear to fin amid nothing, floating in a medium too bright for the mere air of the room, a seraphic atmosphere dispensing light without itself existing in the ordinary sense of things. An emptiness.

My fish rise to the top when I approach. My finger pokes through the surface tension until they caress it with their sides or probing mouths. I know it's greed, but that's what love was at the beginning, and I am content.

At night, their only illumination is the red-glow of the aquarium heater. They're attracted to this, and one can stand in the dark watching ghostly fish circle the dim radiance like forest creatures at the edge of firelight.

I add two black mollies. A mother guppy gives birth, and two babies survive the ravenings of their tank-mates. These hardy remnants bear in them the same elements as I, vomited forth by expiring suns. A Martian chemist would find more similarity between the guppy and me than difference. She would know in an instant that we are children of the same womb. Whether they realize this or not, they plane their scales to the light, catching and diffusing it like a row of tiny blue worlds.

I add sharky scum-suckers, whose Latin name means something like *mouth-on-the-bottom-spiney-one*. They change color. I peer in at morning to find their usual mud-dark transformed to a sandy café au lait. I can do this only on an elementary level, by blushing with mortification or paling with horror.

Their durability amazes and gratifies. A hood's too expensive, so I leave the water open to the air. At morning I find a tetra lying on the carpet. I figure he's been dead for hours, but I dip him in hopefully, and with a jerk that dazzles my hand he's off and away among the plastic weeds. I'd have to work at killing them. Their ancestors preceded mine and taught them a thing or two. I have four limbs because they have two sets of fins. They swagger over the transplanted white creek rocks. I lower my hand into the tank. If I'm patient they come to lie between my fingers. I lift them into my world, into the stinging air. They're no longer what they were: They're—pardon me, but—fish out of water. They jump if I keep them too long, solid insistent muscle, remarkable in such tiny bodies. They are not afraid. They say simply, "Enough."

They regard me dispassionately, but with an understanding of where advantage lies. I am a blur beyond the glass wall of the world, a finger that appears, disappears, is followed by a rain of food. Brush the finger with a crystal fin, food hails down. If I'm run over by a car tonight, they'll gather in the finger-corner, wondering what went wrong until the lights go out. I can hear the fishy Jeremiahs bubbling *Repent!*

I was wrong about fish until I peered through their bones.
My fish.
I come downstairs each morning, astonished that they should still be there. Surely they have other business. Unless I am their business. Unless they stay to teach me something. I think I've learned, but the next day, there they are, faces pressed pityingly against the glass. Surely not just for the pittance of the fish-flakes I shake between my fingers twice a day. I lean close to the water. I think they say *Everything you know is wrong—*
But I am wrong about that too.

❦

I hike Graveyard Fields in blazing light, feeling health and strength. I walk in the creek for a long mile, glad to have placed experience before the safety of my sneakers. Trout dart from me. Butterflies accept me as a careering island in the stream. The water cleanses what it can touch. My feet tingle, massaged, wanting more.

Beauty around me. Beauty under and against me. Happy—not as a blessed spirit, but as an animal, warm in my pelt, beauty and richness gathered to my senses. I take a white stone from the stream, to place it among my aquarium fish, to remember by, to let them travel with me the waters of the Blue Ridge. If the rock were many times heavier I would carry it. They need to know.

That's the second time I hiked Graveyard Fields. The first was last autumn when my friend Kit ventured down from his veterinary practice in New York for a visit. In college he was the strongest man I knew, a varsity wrestler, a marathoner, not large but wiry and handsome and inexhaustible. In graduate school, unlike the rest of us, he widened his interests, becoming a potter, a musician, a poet, and expert in those things that require shaping and consideration. Though we never lost touch, there have been years between our meetings. This didn't bother me, as I assumed we would have a long time to make it up. The world seldom forgives such presumption.

Kit fades slowly now with multiple sclerosis. No longer able to wrestle calves as before, his career as a vet nears its end. Having married a woman who could not go through this tribulation with him, he finds himself not only disabled but abandoned. Insomnia and depression keep him staring at the ceiling through endless nights. His visit was not a happy occasion. I made myself awkward with wondering what to do to make him feel better. He came sad and sick, and our time together was consequently sad until I began to see strength in him that is at once mirth and defiance.

We managed to go hiking. Every step or two I asked, "You all right?" until he told me to shut up.

The day came cool and bright. We picked up a blood path at the parking lot, followed it down a forest road, the blood here thickening when the hunter set its quarry down, there thinning to droplets when the hunter ran. The path crosses Shining Creek at a cluster of deep, clear pools, and in one pool floated a slurry of blood where the creature paused to nibble its prize. A blood-filled organ turned over and over in the bright water, immaculate from the scouring of the current. I touched it before realizing what it was. It burst into a scarlet cloud. Kit thought it might be a spleen. It seemed very large. We imagined the loping mountain carnivore capable of carrying such a prize.

We walked on to a place in the forest that carried the stench of fox. That was likely the hunter, though what the quarry was, we never discovered. Perhaps a fresh road kill found beside the Parkway. There are bobcats in Graveyard Fields, and I longed for it to be one of them. Or a bear, though a creature that size would have left prints in the scant wet earth of the trail.

123

I felt insolently vigorous. I was showing off a little. Kit had always been the athlete; and without awareness of how mean the victory was, I relished climbing where he could no longer climb, running where he had to put his hand on his knee and lean painfully into the slope. It was not intentionally cruel. I don't know that he noticed, or that I would have had I not written it down. The documented life is never innocent.

I played on the edge of a waterfall, effervescent, feeling perhaps with my better self that I could lighten him with my lightness. I sang highlights from the Steeleye Span albums he had played for me long ago. I tried a gazelle leap between rocks. No gazelle, I slipped backward into the water, not afraid until I sensed I couldn't catch myself. The rocks are slippery, the current too deep, too cold, too quick. The river plunges sixty feet onto tumbled boulders, plunges again, and again three times to the valley floor. I was falling. I was going to die.

What happened next was, at the moment, as much a mortification as a miracle. Kit put on the only speed in him, ran, grabbed me, pulled me back onto the rocks. I remember the grip of his hand on my arm, like a god's clench, tranquil and unbreakable.

Yes, I know what it means. And hate it utterly. I'll write nothing until the meaning changes. We have a duty to make it something we can endure.

This was called setting out. This was called the first step.

❦

I had a room with windows on the north and west. Summers I left them open so the wind blew through, toppling knick-knacks from the dresser, swiching the curtains against the walls. Wind carried the scent of Tallmadge marsh and the noise of the farm boys roaring in from Hartville on Saturday night. Stars shone dull from the rubber smoke in the city westward, but I didn't know it could be otherwise and believed heaven was everywhere as I saw it, misty, dichrome ink and pale until the moon rose in its perpetual Halloween.

I'd hear barking. Run to the window. Usually it's just the moon, maddening the vigilance of my black-and-white dog with an imma-

terial invasion, a moon too huge for a boy to cover with his hand
even if he spreads his fingers wide.

Sometimes it's a solitary runner. Dressed in white, he holds his
arms close at his side as though wanting to take up as little of the air
as possible. I guess he lives in the housing project where it floods in
spring and all the houses are made of pastel aluminum. That's the
direction he runs from, padding almost silent toward the city park. A
few dogs, like mine, relieve the night watches with a moment's
barking and a lunge at his shoes. After that he runs alone.

I thought about what he would do running alone in the woods.
Ladies there, made of moonlight, their white hair spread on the
wind. Creatures driven inward by the city long ago. Lost gods, lost
men, derelicts dreaming in the dark until he comes to wake them.

The runner set down his trust while I was away at school. No
one took it up. Tallmadge marsh is a K mart. The five-hilled
wilderness of the park stands hemmed on all sides but one by city
lights.

I will make a visit mean. I'm willing to be late and futile.

I take the solitary runner's old route, going by my window, as he
always did. I do what he did when I was a child wakeful in the blare of
moonlight, peeking behind bedroom curtains. I hold arms tight at
my side. I turn my face from the shrill of the K mart parking lot,
canceling it with disregard.

"*Dogs!*" I yell into back yards if I've run too far unnoticed.

At the Route 91 intersection it's a point of honor not to stop.
You leap across far enough from the cars to be safe, near enough for
effect. A horn or the screech of brakes is a sign of insufficient
elegance. Closeness is perfection, the silent intake of breath, the brake
foot hovering in midair. Leave the driver with tightness at the
bottom of his throat.

Eastwood Road is the lone dark left, its bare field scored with
the tracks of dirt bikes, the blue hulk of the forest on the south side.
The ground isn't level, but not so tilted as to slow me down. I shift
from oncoming headlights less against the glare than not to be
recognized, not to be shouted at and have the spell broken.

That other runner had it easier. Neighborhoods creep close
now: windows to glance into, girls in pairs braving the long bare of
the road in their shorts and T-shirts.

Two girls have convinced the drive-through liquor store clerk that they're of age. It can be done if you're on foot. The clerks are used to handling bottles and change through car windows, and a full-front person puts them off stride. The girls have in their brown bag, I bet, amaretto, to sip in their room or to pour into cola and drink wickedly in the living room in front of their parents. They think themselves bold to be here alone at twilight. Beyond the drive-through liquor store the city fails, no businesses, no houses until Morningview, just the long flank of the park black beside the road.

The girls see me. They lean together to whisper. They turn back to the liquor store. They don't want to be caught between patches of civilization with a strange man loping in white gym shorts. The clerk will think that they have turned back for him.

I try to smile as I pass. My anxiety for the smile not to be a leer makes it one. Whatever expression I wear doesn't feel right on my face. My knees hurt on the uneven ground. I forget my face to concentrate on that. The girls keep walking, arms stiff at sides, eyes forward in an expression meant to convey indifference. It conveys dread and curiosity. Maybe I'm enjoying this. The footpath beside the road is ten feet wide, but they huddle shoulder to shoulder. I hear the dark one say to the tall one, "Don't tell mother!"

I turn onto the park road. It lies bright under the moon.

I feel the girls watch me, like a breeze on the back of my neck. What aren't they going to tell mother? Probably about the liquor, but I hope it's me.

The park road curves by a huge water tower that sings if you touch it. I learned this from a boy who was my friend because his father and mine were friends. He was always telling me things, but that was the only one of use. *Ba-huuuuuuuummmmmm* goes the tower, shivering from the place you strike it clear to the top.

The city fathers built a fence, hating for their handiwork to do anything except what they intended. You can defeat them by remembering to carry stones from the road to hurl in a flying overhand against the resonating drum. *Ba-huuuuummmmm.* Think of the terror by night to one homing late at the wood's edge.

The weeds of the north meadow march steel-colored in the darkness. Hardhack, queen-of-the-meadow, hawkweed, wild rose. A smell like tea steeped all day in a copper kettle. For my Nature Day

Camp kids I made up a story that hawkweed grows where a hawk has killed, a flower sprung from blood and violence. I think it should be true.

I pass little runways of the meadow life, lit by the shimmer of the flat sky, gleam like highways seen from planes. The blind must feel this way, running at the edge of the sea, running by feel, by dead reckoning, by luck. I cross from the open into the forest.

Utterly blind at first, I know the path by memory and navigate after a minute by faint purple radiance from the forest floor. The way is a ribbon of the dimmest conceivable light. Anything could be watching from the underbrush and I wouldn't know. But I hope. I watch for man shape or beast shape rearing in shadow, for a skein of paleness launched in the wind.

I used to be able to sicken myself with thoughts of monsters. This was before I had known anything really terrible. Yet I have never been afraid of the dark, even as a child. Like the Japanese urchin crooning his love-song to Godzilla, I longed for night's children a fraction more than I dreaded them.

Running hard now, confident of footing. I must be bright in this black, a flame, a phantom, with my white shorts and white skin. Maybe the night things hesistate toward me, curious but uncertain. Maybe I'm the one to watch, the apparition loping terribly in the dark. Sweat cools on my chest; I quicken my pace to keep warm.

The path loops down into the pines. Fewer bugs, the fragrance I'd call *Earth* if I smelled it lost in the stars for a thousand years.

Blue before me lies the huge south meadow, mown, knife-stubbled, choking with perfumes, bound southward by Newton Street, which I can reach now in two minutes' run. I race into the field, bounding like an animal to show it I am here. I scan underfoot, where it is silver, to see shoeprints of the solitary runner, preserved as proof that this is the right way. I turn homeward, picking up speed. Pine, oak, into the field of the singing tower. I am going as fast as I ever have, the unevenness of the land rocking my feet left and right. Westward clouds tear, and the young moon snags on the crowns of tulips.

Out on the road, the girls are gone. Speed, speed, all downhill. I whoop at the chained dogs. I watch windows for curtains parting, for eyes of the sleepless trying to see me.

.   .   .

127

I want the watchers to start their explanations here. I want to be at the center, the grit at their pearl's heart.

❦

Monday, climbing the hill to do my laundry, I found an ovenbird sitting on the walk. I picked her up, gently, seeing no wound that could explain her docility. I cradled her in my hands, amazed at her smallness, at her beauty, the greenish-goldish-brown of her back, the electric streaks of dark across her blinding white breast, the subtle crown of sun's-orange, scarcely more than a shimmer of light. She regarded me with black, untroubled eyes. I knew it was a great blessing to hold her, but also that blessings are to be tasted rather than wallowed in, so I set her on a rail and went in to do the wash. In the laundry room sat another ovenbird—her mate, I choose to think—trapped and disoriented. I shooed him through the door. They both fluttered off into the trees.

I know what I'm supposed to think.

Also what I *do* think.

The lease says so clearly "No children" that when I hear them screaming in the parking lot I think I should complain. Not screaming. Laughing. Talking in the low voices of childhood conspiracy. The small ones cry when they tumble onto the pavement. I look through the slats of the blinds at them. They all ride small plastic vehicles with uneven plastic wheels that make noise on the cement like the greatest of tropical rains on a tin roof. The youngest is a boy with a white tricycle. His father rides with him sometimes. He's a photographer for the city paper, with that raggedly, unkempt handsomeness that cameramen seem to have. He rides his ten-speed around his son on his trike for an entire weekend, swiveling and banking so that the boy is never out of his sight. The father speaks to me when I go outside. He says, "You should try this sometime." I don't know whether he means riding a bike around in a parking lot or having a son.

The rest are girls. Two, on the brink of adolescence, seem able to roller skate all day, down stairs, up stairs, across flats and lawns and places where I'd find it hard to walk, let alone roll. I know it's more than skating, but when I watch them to find out exactly what, they turn coy and fade into the doors of their own apartments. They explore. They make up games that involve stealth and reconnaissance. I thought only boys did that, but when I try to think of what girls do instead I come up with dolls and tea parties, things these girls would find unthinkable. Any girls, maybe. I try to learn. When they're out playing I take too long to open my door, walk too slowly to my car. But they're on to me and keep their secrets.

One is fat and loud. One is slender and loud and very beautiful. I don't know which to pity more for what will come. A third girl is much younger and smaller, and the loveliest of the lot. Her red hair flies behind with the effort to keep up with the older girls. Like the tail of a dinosaur, the hair possesses a separate consciousness, wild and nervous, without the inhibitions that hold back the body. She's smarter than the older girls, smarter than most of the people she will ever meet. I talked with her in the laundromat once, and if I closed my eyes and deepened her voice I wouldn't know her from a grown woman of some poise. She doesn't notice that the older girls ignore her. She watches, studies, mimics whatever they do better than they did it. Their relationship is that of a reader to her books, use without engagement.

When I first moved here she had an older brother whom she adored. It was funny to watch her follow him, doubling his gestures like a tiny red shadow. He was a teenager, but like her, small for his age, a wise child bandaged at every corner from precipitous descents from a skateboard. He's gone now, maybe living with their father. I make up stories in which he returns in a long white car and takes her wherever she thinks about when she skates alone in the red hour before night.

Older children dance in the clubhouse above my window. It's hard to see them, but when I do they look like most kids, skinny and funny, wearing oversized shirts in the bright teal that's fashionable now. The lease says so clearly "no children" that when I have to shut my blinds so they can't look straight into my bedroom, I think I should complain. But I ask myself, "Does it really bother you?" and the answer is no. I stand behind the blinds and listen, trying to hear what they laugh at when they laugh.

Two or three times a summer, somebody's exhausted parents send a party of them on a scavenger hunt. I think the parties have something to do with church, for the children are scrubbed and combed and look like their parents would have at such an occassion a third of a century ago. I hear their voices outside considering whether they should bother somebody they don't know. The answer, of course, is no, but they decide it's a worthy cause and ring the bell, asking for green thread and black buttons and matchbooks from restaurants in other states. I watch their faces as they ask, trying to see what they're thinking, trying to remember what I would have thought, if not quite a third of a century, then long enough ago. I listen while they explain, as though I came from a planet where there are no scavenger hunts. I scurry around and find what I have, bringing some of the wrong things to see if they'll take them. When they're gone I leave my porch light on, so the next team will know I'm home and maybe have some green thread left.

I walk under the night sky, hoping for a prodigy, perhaps for a shooting star. I'm good with shooting stars, having seen more than many who stay up late. It has not been a good week. A star might make it okay. If not a star, the wing of a bat against the streetlamp, anything.

Of course there's nothing. I go home, kicking pebbles under my neighbors' cars. Out of all that fullness could have come something. It could have spared me something I could write down and call the meaning of it all. I shake my head, *tsk* for the benefit of invisible auditors. Unlocking my door, I touch my hand to a shrub, pull it away dragging a single green thread.

❧

Found a gray kitten that must in the natural course of things be named Smoky. Put a bowl of skim milk in the grass beside my door, in case it was hungry. Went away, and when I came back, I switched on the light and saw something brownish floating in the liquid, which seemed otherwise untouched. The brown things were the tangled bodies of slugs that had crawled into the milk. The sides of the bowl and the ground around gleamed with the sliding chocolate masses of them. I overturned the bowl, unable to account for my emotion of profound disgust. I got my sack of sea-salt and sprinkled them all, watching while they writhed and shed their skins as though scalded by a blast of steam.

Each night since, I've stayed up late, switched on the porch light, and, catching the gleam of their horrible bodies in the grass, have salted them and watched them die in what even in that dim world must resemble agony. I don't understand my motivation in this. I say, "They destroy vegetation," knowing that that is not the reason.

Steady rain. The earthworms in their myriad of reds and lengths loop the grass, worshipers risen to bathe in the grace of a cool descending god.

I'm glad no one's here to ask why I've been staring at earthworms. In graduate school I worked three nights as a worm gatherer. The bait broker paid five dollars per thousand earthworms. Three nights were plenty. Still, I stare at earthworms while rain gushes down my back.

I want the mud to become crystal. I want to see their flooded houses, the drowned corpses of those who weren't quick enough. I want to feel the blue spark waver in what passes for their brains. I want a clue.

❧

I tried a dozen errands in the morning, all aborted, so I hiked Craggy Gardens, down the long path that leads to Douglas Falls. I ran the whole way down, at peril to bones and to the astonishment of hikers who backed themselves against trees to let me shoot past.

Have taken to running the forest paths. Maybe it'll become a sport, an Olympic event for the foolhardy. It's chancey, but I go slow. You must train your imagination to give your ankles the heft of elephant feet, to be twisted neither right nor left by roots and stones. Keep eyes open. Deer shoot their necks up, unable to believe you come so fast.

I fell twice but lit in such softness of mud and fallen leaves that I wouldn't know I had fallen but for the altered visual perspective.

Came to a beautiful waterfall. I threw a red penny into a pool near the path. Came to another, more beautiful still, whose sheer rock bed was roped off so you don't plunge to the bottom. Neither was "the Falls," so I expect a wonder if I ever return. I'm sweating, and the sweat chills me. I ran again, this time to keep warm.

Two hundred paces farther, in a grove of hemlock and one great cherry, in shadow and holiness, I turned back. I'd run as far as I was going to. I walked, not slowly, but with respect for the uphill grade. Crossed another pair of hikers, and at the first falls saw the penny they threw in to join mine.

Took time for the antics of the juncos, sweet and candid, like new children in the neighborhood who want to come and play but daren't yet; time to look at the jungles of the clubmoss, at perspectives like the painting of a perfect world, mountain after mountain into blue distance. Glad to have the light that last half mile, sun so low and I so high it made a gold lamp at my feet.

Why have I done this?

Ravens stood at the mouth of the path, waiting to celebrate with me, or for the carrion of my failure. I repeat my question for them. They divide the blue air, the sound in their wings like the fall of rain.

❦

You are a Martian voyager. You probe the air of the mountain. Dry and cold and clear, like home. You study the voice of the ravens, listening for mathematical progressions, for equations that split the light from the dark. And you will hear them.

Ravens spiral in cobalt air. They must be blessed spirits, so high and prolonged is their play. They pass close and fast. I know they're black, but they flash and sparkle in the light. The noise of their wings is a flight of arrows, a boy switching a green wand through the air.

I've always thought of flight as silent. It is certain the birds do not.

❦

Every detail recorded as though it will be the keystone, the completion of the arch. I gather like Joseph's pharoah against the day of famine. I want to know, don't know how except to hold to everything.

Shining Rock Wilderness.

Hike Ivestor Ridge in a blaze of cold blue light.

Mountains took time to impress themselves on me. People would say, "Look at the mountains," and I did, without the emotion implied by their voices. My landscape is gentle—not a place tourists come to for snapshots, but one revealing beauty and intricacy at close inspection: the speckles of a salamander's back, the gills of mushrooms, a frill of leaves.

But I see them now, the mountains, hiding behind immensity.

Ivestor Gap opens on a hundred animal-shaped mountains, multi-colored, crowned heads in the sun, gigantic and inhuman, vistas sweeping and crossing and vanishing in distance, no particular thing, but a presence of vastness and power, crushing and uplifting at once, the atmosphere so pure that I and the ravens seem to be the only things alive in it.

Dance on the broken rocks of the road.

Climb bald Grassy Top, focused down Ivestor Gap like a bridegroom eternally on the body of his sleeping bride. The slopes of the mountain whip in the gale, but the top sits calm, the trees and grasses almost motionless. On the lee side I find a tiny rain forest, spruce, hemlock, rhododendron dripping damp onto a floor of moss. I leave a new penny in the crotch of a tree to mark the far point of my passage.

What does it mean, what does it mean—the chant goes on in my head, though I understand that it is not right to ask.

Climb down with my ankles aching. Climb down with sun in my eyes until clouds spill over the mountain crests: heavy gray men who barely made it to the top and mean to scurry down the other side at ease. Rays pour through tears in tumbling clouds.

Find a stocking cap dropped by one of the hunters I'd passed earlier. Tall men. They were wary of me, though they had the guns. They jumped when I spoke to them. The cap is sky-blue, and I put it on. Too small. I hang it on a thorn for the next passer-by.

At distance I see my little silver car in the silver of the clouds, as though floating in midair.

Probe Sleepy Gap, the sky clear and blue to the point of eeriness. Walk in a deep valley, the hearth of a ruined cabin here, a singing water there. This is a managed forest, and if I deduce correctly from the evidence, "managed" means mown down to improve hunting. It's all right. It improves sightlines too, and I see hills pass as rounded and orderly as knobs on a crocodile's back.

I'm alone, a mote moving in a blaze of crystal. An ocean, a deep substance—of what? Light? Oxygen? Like the water of my fish tank, sometimes effulgent but not demonstrably present, sometimes as palpable as beaten silver. Hunters huddle together, awkward and radiant, like newborn gods. I stand at the bottom of the valley, gazing past the encircling mountains, able to think that the fire was lit and the azure hung for me. Surely it was lit and hung, and here I stand, drinking it alone, little yellow Adam in the garden before Eve. Greed and satiety and delight. One soul to stand before the countenance of God.

Sit, immobile with warmth and walking and contentment. Beauty a wand of flame, a roof of blazing sapphire. I curl on a stone amid running water, asleep like a lizard in the flood of gold.

❧

I'm waiting for the moment. I send out my little probes, thicken the sheaf of paper on the shelf, jam my floppy disks. I walk grimly on the ridge, wanting to go home. *All right,* I say to the mountain, *show me something.*

I save Shining Rock itself for Easter Sunday. I want to stand at its top at dawn. I want to huddle there alone when the sun blazes over Ivestor Ridge. I draw my jacket around me against the upland cold.

In the light, finally, I see why it is called Shining Rock. This is a mountain made of crystal, sometimes pink, sometimes purplish or golden, but overwhelmingly white. Ivory. Snow. Quartz. Moonlight. I fill my pockets with pure white stone, longing for them, hungry to possess a fragment of a holy place. After half a mile on the homeward hike I'm sweating and exhausted. I empty my pockets, making a little heap of snow-colored stones under the green laurel.

Easter. I run, empty-pocketed, light as air. I see now. To bring the fragments home was not the point at all. A whole crystal range, or vacancy.

You are a Martian scientist. You have gone fishing. You haul up a line of unimaginable length, at the end of which dangles a trap, a little box of wonders dredged from the third planet. You anticipate vapor, dust, a needle of quartz.

You open.

In the first three seconds of glory, eyes, heart, tongue are burned away.

Curlews

W e are immortal until the hour death first seizes our imagination. This goes for species as well as individuals. To die you must once consider death and think of it as beautiful. All spiritual advances are advances in aesthetics.

The cockroach, the horseshoe crab have never quite come to grips.

❦

Easter that year was as early as it could be. Wind blustered from the flatlands by Lake Erie, blowing the tan dust of winter's end into nostrils and eyes. There were no flowers except for what the deacons brought from the florist shop on Pioneer Street. Dust scoured a flowerless flat land, all under dry gold light that rubbed even the dust and the bareness ringing clean. Emmanuel Church was not beautiful so much as lively and expectant, its walls stark behind the store-bought lilies. Deacons and elders wore black winter suits, their tight smiles expressing Dutch Reformed abashment before an indecorous feast, neither Protestant nor Northern. Only the boy's mother wore anything like an Easter bonnet, because he begged her to, a pink dome surrounded by a corona of pale flowers and small, hard fruit. It didn't matter that she removed it the moment she entered the building; the boy was satisfied.

The boy knew how things were meant to be even when he'd never seen them himself. He read everything. He listened to the conversations of adults with reptilian attention. He knew when they were wrong, and also that to be told they were wrong irritated them, and when therefore to keep silent. He knew that Easter Sunday required bright bonnets of the women. He knew that he himself should have a new suit, though he seldom did, and that it should be a gay color like green or cream. He knew that there should be flowers, not only from the florist but also covering the world in commemoration of the miracle.

Though he found no proof, he suspected that his church picked the wrong date for Easter. Deliberately. Out of an unaccountable impulse to ruin. He remembered three or four Easters, and there were never flowers, not real ones from the ground. Sleet. Cold. Nothing pertinent to resurrection except the blazing acid light.

Easter meant Jesus had been dead three days, then rose and was alive. The boy made sure of that point, asking again and again, "And it means that after three days Jesus rose from the dead, and *that* means after three days *we* rise from the dead?" And they told him, *Yes*.

Much of the world was mysterious, and there was no way of telling what was really a mystery and what was obscured by the confusion of the people who had to be asked. When he could, the boy found out things on his own. When he didn't know how, as a final recourse he asked adults, never quite trusting the answers but hoping at least for a clue to send him to the right place from which to continue on his own.

The three days seemed doubtful, or at least incomplete. It was too mathematical. Adults were always leaving things out of their explanations, sometimes because they didn't know better, sometimes because they didn't realize that he truly needed to know. So he asked again about the three days, and again they told him that's how it was, that's what Easter stood for.

"Does this have to begin on Good Friday and end on Easter, or can it be any Friday and any Sunday, or can it be any three days at all?"

They said it could be any three days at all. This news sat in his heart. His reason for asking was the body in the field on Good Friday.

The boy's father had taken him kite flying on Good Friday. There was something wrong with this. He wanted to sit and think about death and Jesus—not out of morbidity, but because what he read and fragments he heard spoken in tones of awe or embarrassment by aged, odd people at church told him it was right to do so. In a book a saint had done this, and when he had done it very long, God put blood into his hands and feet. But he knew already what could and couldn't be said to adults, what they would accept, what expressed desires would make them force on him their opposite.

Light came dry, golden, the wind behind it, a kite-upholder. He squirmed to think what they would say if he told them what he wanted.

His father seemed sure that March was kite time. This had the ring of ritual that the boy loved, so he said yes to kites, a white one, unfigured, a holy blankness in the Easter. His father got a red kite with prints of fighter planes with teeth at the front like tigers.

They drove to the open field across from the metropolitan park, thirty acres free of wires and trees. Others flew already, and the boy thrilled that his father had been right. There was still room in the sky. Blue kites, red, yellow, box kites like the stuffed, bright-colored garbage bags that blow wild on windy nights before pick-up day. Not one was white. His father had been right again.

As soon as he got out of the car, the boy saw the puppy in the ditch at the roadside. His father told him to get away from it, and he handed him the kite.

"What killed it?"

The dog didn't look smashed, but his father thought that it might have been a car. He said, "Get away from there."

"How long has it been dead?"

"Not long. Now get away." His father said he had to run to get the kite into the air.

His father wanted him to forget the puppy lying dead at the roadside. The boy knew he couldn't push much further. If he wanted to know more, he would have to ask later, when his father wouldn't suspect he was thinking of the corpse.

The body was gold. He wanted to scrape it once with the toe of his shoe to see if it was the puppy's color, or the dust that settled everywhere, invisible until it came to the ground, swirling in tiny cyclones over the grass. The boy ran, paying string out behind until the kite leapt into the air.

His father had answered, "Not long." How long was that? Two days? One? Just since that morning? While he stood at the end of the tugging kite string, he wondered if things must die on Friday to rise up on Sunday. He wanted to see the puppy rise. He couldn't ask then, knowing he would be told to get such things out of his mind, but when at church the matter seemed appropriate, he asked, and they said rising comes three days after any day, and it didn't matter anymore if the puppy died on Thursday or Friday.

The boy wanted to see the puppy rise from the dead. His faith was a torrent, a pale crown levitating over his head. He'd go back when the puppy had gone to heaven, on the third day. He had no doubt.

The next morning he went with his mother to the supermarket because he knew she would pass the kite field, and she would stop and let him look if he said he had lost something. She stopped, far from the puppy, so the boy ran at the field's edge, pretending to search for something the location of which he knew exactly. It lay where it had lain before, its belly swollen, flies on its exposed eye. He didn't slap at the flies, which might be part of the miracle.

"When Jesus rises on the third day, is it right at the beginning, right at dawn?"

She told him, *Yes*. He'd come to the field Sunday, and the puppy would be gone.

Easter that year was as early as it could be. Dry and cold. The men stood with their cigarettes in front of the church, thin hair blowing backward from their heads. The boy sensed they didn't altogether like a day to make its own rules, to complicate a matter otherwise as predictable and as steadfast as death, but they had to mention it was Easter, had to admit to the miraculous one day in the year. The boy felt a secret shared between himself and God. One day when they told him not to worry about such things at his age he would answer, *I know. I already know.*

The boy considered not going to the field to look. It was possible a sanitation truck had picked the body up, but then it would rise from the bed of the sanitation truck, or from the silvery detritus of the landfill. He was certain. He held faith in the center of his brain like a yellow jewel. Like the saint in the book, but better somehow, because bloodless and secret.

Only uncertainty as to what would manifest faith more fully made him ask to go kite flying in the afternoon. He didn't need proof, but he had begun to believe he was meant to bear witness. Not to prophesy, but if asked, to answer, *Yes, I know.*

The wind had never stopped, and on the near horizon they could make out kites already soaring over the golden field. He would stand on the spot where the puppy had been, and people would see or not. But he would know.

His father was surprised by the request, perhaps delighted by its normality; and so with Easter ham and spiced apples in their bellies they went to the bright field to play.

They parked near enough to where they had parked before so that the boy, though he meant to delay and savor the discovery, caught the puppy in the corner of his eye almost immediately. By running very fast and very far from the spot, he was able to convince himself he had seen nothing, or if he had, it was a temptation to disbelief and not the untenanted roadside that must really be there. Closer and closer the boy circled with the kite line jerking through his hand, wanting to plunge in the updraft. The flatness of the meadow was such that far off he still couldn't avoid seeing the puppy. Hoping it might be a test of faith, he ran to its side, not looking at it directly, because his father was watching and would know why he had wanted to come to the field. The swelling in its belly had deflated, and a few bones showed through the digesting pelt. The eyes were eaten away. It was dead. Plain dead. It had not risen Easter morning.

His father was looking, so he ran to the center of the field, trying to think at once about the dog and about not tangling the others' strings. The boy ran with the kite string tight in his hand. Even when his father called him, he ran a little farther, to the fence that must be the field's end. The wind never wavered. Gold, bright, cold. Always the fine dust ready to be tasted if he opened his mouth.

The boy was crying. He had never felt sorry for the puppy until that moment, its being dead under the yellow dust. He ran back to his father, reeling in string so they could go home.

❧

You are a twelve-year-old boy. You're in love with creatures vanished from the world before the fathers of your fathers dropped from the trees. I don't mean interested in them. I mean in love, so night and morning pass with their lumbering mysteries of bodies still processing, stately and hopeless, through your dreams. Why? Why would you walk out of this world without regret if the door opened on the endless garden of former time?

Genesis tells two creation stories. In the first, God says, "Be fruitful and multiply, and replenish the earth, and subdue it: and have dominion over the fish of the sea, and over the fowl of the air, and over every living thing that moveth upon the earth."

The second: "And the Lord God took man, and put him into the garden of Eden to dress it and keep it."

One a conqueror, one a gardener. Even the Gods are different, one speaking the ineffable Word of creation, the other kneeling on the riverbank, kneading man out of dust, breathing into his nostrils the breath of life. It's a division that persists in the human heart. The day we took our destinies in our hands—by fire, medicine, technology, longing, will—we left the path of the animals. It is a grievous thing, but no sane person wants to go back. We are not part of nature. Genesis recognizes us our alternatives: lords of creations or shepherds of creation.

That "lord" should mean, inescapably now, "despoiler" is an aspect of the Fall.

You are Adam. The Lord God listens while you name the creatures, nodding His cloudy head in assent. It takes a long time, but you *have* a long time. When you finish, He says, "These may be your brothers or your servants. If your brothers, their destiny will be your destiny. If your servants, fear must grow between you. They will flee, and you will destroy them. Choose."

Pigs, rats, goats, cats introduced into a previously isolated ecosystem can cause environmental disaster. Many indigenous Polynesian species are either extinct or threatened beyond reasonable hope of recovery.

In uninhabited areas, wildlife is often tame and unafraid. Guns are not necessary. They walk into your hands.

On one island an entire species of bird was wiped out in a few years by a lighthousekeeper's cat.

After recovering from near-extinction by the fur trade, the sea otter finds itself threatened again by fishermen who blame it for a dramatic decrease in the abalone harvest. Though proof exists that the abalone beds were decimated by silt from the construction of the Pacific Coast Highway, the sight of another mammal with a salable commodity in its paws drives us wild.

The American Army gave Plains Indians blankets taken from smallpox wards. Smallpox, an Old World disease, went through the native population like wildfire.

In pioneer Ohio, especially around Hinckley and in the Western Reserve, a series of stupendous hunts was organized to clear the area of "dangerous" animals. Hundreds of men formed a circle in the forest and drove the game to a cleared space in the center, where others stood with loaded rifles. One hunt in Freedom in 1818 bagged 20 bears, 11 wolves, 700 deer, an uncalculated measure of wild turkeys and assorted game. The bounty of the land was so great that it could support this sport for several years.

In the 1820s, British authorities detoured shipments of food away from the starving Irish on the grounds that charity would encourage dissolute ways.

In the cliffs of Moher on the west coast of Ireland nests the kittiwake, a gull with an especially piercing and disturbing cry. Legend has it that the kittiwake learned its cry from starving people who in desperation climbed the cliffs looking for birds' eggs and fell screaming to the sea below.

Half of all species of plants and animals on dry land live in the tropical rain forest. This stupefying diversity arises, probably, from the fact that the tropics have been the tropics for a very long time. While glaciers marched over the rest of the world and oceans invaded and retreated in response to their moods, the tropics sat relatively untouched, multiplying their grandeur and abundance. Every square inch is a garden. Every furlong teems with prey and predator, from the patient devouring fungal spore to the gliding jaguar.

Since World War II, half the tropical jungles of the world have disappeared. The few that remain dwindle hourly. Some are cleared for highways or farms. Most are ground down for pulpwood, a unique biota transformed into used-car ads in the morning paper. As a generation, we preside therefore over the mass extermination of half the species of the earth, a holocaust unparalleled since the cancellation of the dinosaurs.

We are already culpable for the extinction of the great herd mammals of the Pleistocene, which, surviving Ice Age well enough, could not cope with the growing efficiency of our ancestors' hunting methods. Mammoth, mastodon, giant bison, aurochs, ground sloth, American camel, American horse, Irish elk—the list is long and dreary.

The speed of extinction of the North American biota is almost incredible until one realizes that they had never seen men, an invading Old World species.

The mammoth looked up, then went back to grazing. No fangs, no claws—what danger could it be?

The ground sloth sat with placid, curious eyes trained on the ape, until it plunged its spear into them.

In the Jewish ghettos during World War II—well, you see the point.

.   .   .

None of these incidents is especially shocking from the viewpoint of natural selection. Nor, of course, what is meant by it.

❦

The voice said, "Cry."
And he said, "What shall I cry?"
"All flesh is grass, and the goodliness thereof is as the flower of the field. The grass withereth, the flower fadeth, because the spirit of the Lord bloweth upon it. Surely the people is grass."
"The grass withereth, the flower fadeth: but the word of our God shall stand forever."

It is a mistake to think that evolution is not suggested in Holy Writ. Selection as well, though one hesitates to say "natural" selection; the selection Isaiah has in mind is supernatural, but with the mystery and unintelligibility of any horrific natural event.
It is a further mistake to think of mankind as a special case. *Behold, they are all vanity: their works are nothing: their molten images are wind and confusion.*

Eve's acceptance of the fruit is an allegory of self-consciousness, a far-off memory of the moment when a promising ape became Homo sapiens. The voice of God walking in the cool of the garden cries out plaintively, "Who told you you were naked?" Nobody told us. You woke us, Lord, animals. We bed down tonight, men.

❦

Ancient man possessed an instinctive grasp of orderly natural succession. Pharoah dies, but there is always pharoah. Assyrians lay down their ravenings: Hittites or Parthians come to take their place. A dozen divinities preside over Delphi, but it remains the omphalos. The divinities themselves flower from ice-exhaling thunderers into Christs and Buddhas. Solomon says, "There is nothing new under the sun." He does not say, "There is no *one* new." The individual passes away; the set, the category persists. Dynasty trails dynasty, boasting empire after boasting empire, always a dynasty, always an empire, though the works of individuals become wind and confusion.

On the plain surrounding Ur, jackal and lion assume ecological niches once filled by gleam-eyed hunting packs of the Pleistocene. The graceful cheetah of the Persian kings prances out from the skin of monsters with the heft of bears. Abraham culls his flock from the unicorns of Eden.

Like kings from a Mesopotamian chronicle, these rulers of a former world leave behind a few relics and a pedigree of jaw-cracking names.

Over in America, camels herd with caribou, saber-toothed cats stalk elephants, killing less with a stab than with a terrible raking parallel to the victim's body, destroying skin and muscle, staining the snow with blood. Ten tons of sea-cow plough the waters of the north Pacific. Hammurabi, or even George Washington, could have seen these had he sailed to the Komandorskiye Islands. Steller's sea-cow will survive until 1768, when Russian sealers exterminate it twenty-seven years after discovering it. Whatever lumbering kelp-gobbler of the Cretaceous it replaced vanished unlamented by either ecologists or sentimentalists.

Backward through the epochs, other predators, other prey: nightmare rattites kicking the guts from proto-antelope; bi-pedal sprinting razors, part bird, part dinosaur, part bad dream, bringing down their victims in a *Götterdämmerung* of reptile flesh.

The planet probably didn't notice the difference. Until quite recently, to consider extinction was to consider the extinguishment of a particularity, never of a destiny. Except to the morbidly specialized, the distinction between a Sargon and a Babur is academic. Likewise, leopard and tyrannosaur are, in a planetary context, the same animal, performing the same labor. Nut-cracker, bone-gnawer, nectar-sipper are eternal classifications. The particular inhabitant of these niches is temporary and contingent. Because the spirit of the Lord bloweth upon it, one nectar-sipper vanishes, another creature rises to seize this honor formerly undreamt.

There is always the potentate, always the spoiler, always the messiah, though names change and grass grows over the capitals.

.   .   .

Those whom this horrifies have an ally in the shortness of human life, the longest of which takes in only a ripple of the long convulsion.

Many modern species are absolutely certain to become extinct in the wild within this century.

Cousin chimpanzee and his neighbors are threatened by an African population explosion. Until recently the human population of this continent—by best guess the race's homeland—was controlled by disease and famine. Modern medicine and advanced agricultural technology enable it to support many more people than it ever has before. The undeniable improvement in human welfare is tempered, perhaps, by the recognition that banana plantations will grow where gorillas napped in the sun, that roads will cut the wildebeest from million-year-old migration routes.

Does this bother you? If so, do you feel ashamed, a traitor to your species?

I hit the remote-control channel button when television nature programs begin to whine about impending natural holocaust. Next to religion, Communism, and The Decline of the Family, it is the topic most likely to induce hysteria in the educated American adult. Hundreds of species *are* in peril of their lives. Unlike Pleistocene hunters, we do not stampede whole herds of aurochs and wild ass over cliffs into our larders, but we destroy habitat, which if less spectacular is incalculably more dangerous. This swamp is drained, that meadow asphalted over—true, but I don't want to hear it always. Sometimes I need the illusion of Eden. When I hear the voice of God walking in the cool of the garden, I want to have an answer for Him. Either "I am innocent, Lord" or, "It was my destiny." I'm at a loss as to what else can be done short of the most radical revision of man's view of himself in the world.

Yahweh must be induced to rescind the terrible words, "have dominion over the fish of the sea, and over fowl of the air..."

How likely is that? The words are delicious. They deliver unto us the desire of our hearts.

The futility and confusion of alternatives makes discussion burdensome.

Some would have it this simple: Either human babies eat, or the wild continues to exist. Of course it's not that simple, but no matter. To quibble against the lives of the babies is unthinkable, or at least unsayable.

It's a Pleistocene reaction: either us or them.

❦

Nevertheless, my fantasies brim: Transfigured trees of Brazilian rainforests magically resist ax and flame. Nothing harms them. They creep into the cities, over the farms, rattling flowers like sabers against the stars.

A mysterious genetic hiatus over a generation or so reduces the human population to a supportable billion. Lianas climb abandoned tenements. Bison scratch their backs on rusted tractor-trailers. We in our condensed but unspeakably beautiful cities cherish one another the more for our rarity. We daytrip among lions and giraffe. We stand at the sea's edge, singing back to great whales. There needn't be so many of us, as we are not lonely anymore.

The poacher's gun backfires. Whalers sink at harbor's mouth. The interstate sinks under cattails; swallows nest in the tollbooths. The basements of subdivisions hiss with rising water. Loons cry in the Hudson. Plutonium alchemizes to gold in the crucible of the warhead.

If I were God I would attempt these things. Being who I am, I shrug and say that there have always been deaths. Every 26 million years or so come extinctions so thorough and catastrophic as to appear complete. We recover. The remnant species radiate. Sea and forest fill. The beasts of the field stand motionless with plenty. I say these things with the wry smile you wear when you tell a child at her first heartbreak, "Everything will come out all right." You know it won't.

What you mean is that something will survive.

And there are surprises.

As a child I was fascinated by coelacanth, that blue-scaled lobe-fin fish finning back from the dead into the waters off Madagascar. I longed with great longing to see it fathoms deep in living water. I still do.

I lived to hear rumor of the ivory-billed woodpecker alive in Cuba.

Some sober scientists do not instantly discount tales of brontosaurs in African lakes, of unnamed pinnipeds in the murk of Loch Ness. We wear coelacanth on our foreheads like *tefillin*.

No, I do not believe in living dinosaurs, or secret mountain hominids, or sea serpents, or UFOs—yet were I to encounter one, my surprise would not be unbearable. And the emotion might not be surprise at all.

🐦

Once I saw a ghost.

Winter light fell on the Texas coast. I walked backward, not so you could see, but in time, counting the years with each step. I went out from motel lobby and beach flotsam, from among pale vacationers exercising their dogs on the sand—sand ground from the bodies of creatures dead before the empires of the world began. I hugged the breakwall that keeps the hurricane out sometimes. Meadowlarks gurgled on the wires, fresh and sun-colored, new mintage in an old world. I found the marsh road and took it as far back as it was going, into a land filled with tiny voices, with low metallic ponds darkened by waders. I retreated from the present into a past so past that I thought I might see something no eye had seen for a million years.

Believe me that these things are possible, if only one could desire enough, long enough, wisely enough, if one could find the right vibration of will to shatter the barriers.

The sand yielded under my feet. It wore the color of pale butter, of a cougar's pelt. It took the shape of whatever last passed over it—a breeze, the highest tide ripple, the claws of birds. My own tracks followed me like the spoor of a dinosaur. I do not remember ever being so observant as then. Perhaps it was the air, neither warm nor cold, so perfectly adjusted to my body as to be impalpable. A meadowlark gurgling in a bush quickened my pulse. I whirled for the shadows of gulls, too huge and silent to be what they were. I believed it to be a day on which I would know something wonderful.

What came of it was the vision of two curlews on Galveston Island. They were quite distinct, one smaller and shorter-billed than the other at a season when size differential is not likely to be the result of age. I knew the larger immediately as *Numenius americanus*, the common long-billed American curlew; but because of the magic of the day, because of the strangeness of winter light, I hoped the other might be *Numenius borealis*, the Eskimo curlew, a bird rare to the point of the fabulous.

By the word of some, then, extinct.

I'd flown to Houston to attend the convention of the Modern Language Association, an experience not unlike a stroll among the nervous waders of the Gulf. In the whistling vacancy of the Houston Hyatt Regency dwelt the biota of a profession: unspecialized starling-like creatures darting into whatever controversy became available, propounding Bentham one moment and Dante the next, ears cocked for scavenge, advancement, or, sometimes, knowledge; hyperspecialized library fowl sipping nectar from a single flower only, evolved to precise and brilliant focus, able to say all that's sayable concerning Dryden's use of the tercet, liable to extinction at the burning of a single book; ambitious cuckoos and raucous jays letting the unformed children of their brain be fed into maturity by others, thieving merrily and holding their prizes up for inspection at the next California cash bar; high-flying hunters, swift to the mark, the hawks and storm-riding Canadas approaching at great height and great speed, taking in whole quarters of the world.

After a few days of that particular exhilaration I felt the need for contrast. I skipped the penultimate session of the convention and took a bus to Galveston for my first look at the Gulf of Mexico. I don't remember anything but brown scrub of identical shape and dimension between Houston and Galveston, though I'll grant that late December may not be that land's best season.

I longed to see an armadillo—even a dead one smashed at the roadside—and kept nose glued to the window, but I was not fulfilled.

The bus made stops at the fringes of Texas City. What I knew of the town was that once it had blown up. It's the sort of thing I'd love to see for myself if I could work out the moral intricacies.

Egrets stab and stalk in the shadow of refineries, gas flares flickering over their crests. I suspect the refineries photograph them and call it an example of the compatability of nature and technology. I feel it is a momentary grace.

Galveston I liked for its mixture of fine Victorian architecture and personable tumble-down informality. I bought a sandwich and was called "hon" three times by people who didn't know me from Adam. I bought a map. On part of the map stood the streets and blocks and points of interest of Galveston. Beyond it lay a great blank dotted with the blue of tide pools. It was that blank I wanted.

A concrete sea-wall defends the city from the gulf, and the frontier-created windward of the wall brims with bird life and creeping things that the punctilious would, I suppose, call vermin. The beach had become a sort of highway for off-road vehicles and motorbikes, and for safety's sake one walked close to the water, sidling into the wavelets when some horsepowered hot dog gunned too close.

On the public beach, sanderlings pattered in and out of the surf on their clown feet, at once hilarious and, against that immensity of water, brave and solemn. One grass-green hermit crab had chosen a shell of deep sandy crimson to an effect of flawless elegance.

What from a distance looked like boulders turned out to be rubber tractor tires buried in the sand, gleaming black in the waves. Sacks of bright plastic components washed up beside sea-monstery lengths of rubber hose, boots, an unruffled copy of *Sports Illustrated*. A huge clear bag full of tiny seashells settled on the tiny seashells of the shore. The effect of all that trash was curiously beautiful, the flotsam of Atlantis tossed up, cleansed and mysterious.

I turned inland toward the U.S. Fish and Wildlife laboratory lagoon, startling a blue heron that deigned to flap a few yards before landing and going on with its hunt.

The theory that birds are dinosaurs shrunk, feathered, and shot into the sky is never more believable than in clear view of a heron, with its reptilian eye, its un-avian immensity and croak, its air of the primeval. I watched it long and close, a disturbing experience, one that made me a little afraid. I wouldn't have wanted a closer look even had the bird granted it. My apprehension was not physical, but something sprung from the otherness of the creature stilting about in the lagoon twenty feet away. Only by accident did we dwell in the same world. I was watching time.

Death did not seize whatever passed for the dinosaurs' imagination. Far from it. They pulled the greatest trick of creation to avoid it, a vanishing act so subtle and intricate we only now come to an appreciation. They transfigured, stoked their furnaces, sped up their hearts, climbed into their disguises, leapt into the air. The Aztecs with their feathered serpent had looked into the heron's eye.

What did the heron see as she caught me in the yellow moon of her eye? Time, perhaps, but what time? The future? A fleeting, imperiled present moment, a figure small and vivid, an emperor looked at through the wrong end of a telescope?

My concentration on the heron was so great that I didn't notice the Virginia rail hunting at my sneaker tips. I laughed aloud with the relief of seeing her merry in the sedges, poking and probing, wading boldly to the center of the lagoon, but never so far that the westering sun left her in too high a relief against the water. I don't think I could have spooked her with anything less than a buck-and-wing. I moved freely, chattering to her. I contend that she paused and listened. Never quailing before the specter of anthropomorphism, I say that the rail's expression was much closer and more readable than the heron's, and what it expressed was satisfaction. One salt pond is world enough.

Across the dirt road shone a much larger pond, where visibility was reduced, paradoxically, by the superabundance of light, for it lay between me and the crisp winter sun. Glare from it flashed golden and tremendous. But I could see that it was strewn with the shadows of waders. I edged down to the shore. In the shining I seized on the unmistakable silhouette of a curlew. To the curlew's left and nearer to me stood another shadow, like the curlew's, but smaller, just over half its size, not a whimbrel, not a—what else was there? My heart leapt at the thought that I might be seeing the Eskimo curlew.

I took a chance that these birds would be infected with the casualness of the rail and the heron. I crept along to get a vantage point with the sun out of my eyes. The birds did not move: tame from protection in a federal lagoon, or perhaps for that hour charmed. I knew that the same light which blinded me must be lighting me up like a Christmas tree, inching in a ludicrous charade of inconspicuousness on their shore. I reached a shaded angle, whipped out my camera, swiveled the lens onto the bird. Too far. Though I could see well enough now, the curlews shrunk to sticks in the viewfinder. Had to get closer, wade into the pond if necessary.

That was a mistake. The instant sneaker touched water, the birds flew, calling, the little curve-bill shearing off from the path of the big one, and I too busy fishing myself from the drink to watch where they had gone.

On top of everything I had read the schedules wrong and arrived as my bus belched toward the Houston road. I had to run ignominiously to catch it, had to sit sweaty and breathless and unable to share the tale of my travels back through time.

"I saw a bird," I might say.

They would smile, turn half to the window, wanting to be left to their own thoughts.

"An *Eskimo curlew!*"

They'd smile, turn fully now to watch the toss of refinery lights on egret-y water.

I returned home on New Year's Eve, where, researching my bird books, I discovered that the last reliable sighting of the Eskimo curlew had indeed been on Galveston Island. I called the local Audubon hierarchy, whose opinion was that it was the wrong time of year for a sighting, and if the poor thing existed at all it would be padding the shores of Patagonia.

That news did not convince me I had not seen the bird. It convinced me I might have seen something more amazing still.

You've had the experience of talking with a friend in a bookstore or on a street corner, and late in the night the phone rings to tell you he is dead. Tidings of the curlew moved me in the same way. Had I seen the last one on Earth, who chose to pass his days in peace on

155

that prow of sand rather than risking Patagonia a final, futile time? I cherished the possibility that I had seen the shade of a creature already fading from memory.

Extinct is an oddly clinical word. A mishap, it sounds, a slip of the evolutionary pen. The word does no justice to a calamity exceeding imagination. I thought I would be content even if I knew the curlew beyond doubt to be extinct, content to have seen the ghost of a bird where it flourished in life, passing as hesitantly from its home as human ghosts are said sometimes to pass from theirs.

I went to Houston to get a university teaching job. I did not get one. Usually I resent having to think of good things as compensation for greater things denied, but the curlew, this time, was enough.

To this tale there is a coda. I heard early in 1982 of an unmistakable sighting and identification of the Eskimo curlew. The news made the experience a little less mystical, if much happier. There remained the possibility that I had seen the real bird, a notch on my life list to be clucked over with a superior air and a lyrical memory of a sandy island bathed in winter light.

And if a ghost, it had been no flickering shade, but a tough little spirit of determination guarding its clawhold of Texas sand, death no more in its mind than it is in mine, or even less.

❦

I have, of course, wanted the ordinary things. But I have also desired with a full and Faustian heart to lay eyes on the creatures of vanished eras. I covet time machines wildly and irrationally, from Dr. Who's tardis to a self-generated crystal bubble that turns the spot on which I stand backward in history. Any spot will do, for it's not human history I mean. Napoleon and St. Paul interest me only marginally. But I ache from my marrow to see diplodocus shoulder among the tree-ferns. This is not curiosity. It is love unfulfilled, unrequited, an obsession as gaudy as a Tudor tragedy. I want to stand on Pangea's shore and watch the swan-necks fishing, the great fins at their harvest in the deep.

Sometimes it seems possible. How remote can something be on this little world? If I could wrinkle time....If I could part the veil....

That the animals do not participate in salvation is a particularly myopic prejudice. Who are the elder children of the world? Whom has God preserved longest?

Giant ground sloths became extinct so recently that in caves in Terra del Fuego their pelts have been mummified recognizably by the freeze-drying atmosphere, hair and fatty tissue intact.

Members of the Russian nobility once dined, in a memorable passage of human pride, on mammoth meat preserved in the high Arctic. People now living heard in childhood possibly genuine eyewitness reports of the New Zealand moa.

That one now living will—barring some millennial alteration of attitude—be the last person on Earth to see a wild rhino or a free-living orangutan fills me with a rage more immediate, but substantially identical. Something belonging to me and my descendants has been stolen away, and there is no court from which to petition redress.

Clark Reservation in upstate New York is a tiny wilderness preserve surrounding a glacial plunge pool. A plunge pool forms when a waterfall, possibly a mile high, dives from the thawing face of a glacier. In the rock of the cliffs lie ghostly pale shells, fossils of a sea that tossed under the moon and vanished. Conceivably a billion years lie between them and me, yet I touch them, imagine them gleaning the bounty of that elder world. Such chronicles render ordinary aspiration vain. I want to die in a shallow, cool sea, near the mouth of a river, where my bones may be silted under, the decomposing bacteria smothered. I want the continent to drift until the ice grinds down to uncover me, that eyes might see and wonder 50 million generations hence. Now *that's* an ambition.

❦

There's a series of alternate Paradises in which I would feel at home. They are all, I see now that I sit down to write of them, sprung from unfulfilled longing.

You are Adam, and this is the Garden of the World, the blue Ark plowing its ellipse among the stars. Cycads scrape the clouds. A clutch of dragon's eggs gleams like ruby on the riverbank. You hear

God walking in the cool of the morning. He brings beasts. He asks their names. You say, "Panther." You say, "Bird of Paradise." The panther scampers to the golden plain, where, pursuing impala, he crosses the paths of the stalking allosaurs. The smilodons roar, and God giveth them their meet in due season.

The bird of paradise flutters up between the calm chomping faces of giraffe and indricotherium. The father of crocodiles gleams agate and malachite on the riverbank. Mosasaur and dolphin sport in the breakers. Ramapithecus croons to her daughter in the araucaria shade.

The matrix of the world lies round about so rich you think nothing could harm it. Who can raise his hand against the thunderers, the sea-lords, the shakers-of-the-earth? Yet you have seen visions, heard voices whisper in the flowering groves. They have told you that one death, like a single pearl broken from a diadem, changes everything. The right death—that unsuspected bacterium, a lowly worm, an unconsidered grass—and the plains empty, the riverbank goes dark. So long as you dwell in paradise, this knowledge, like a fantastic tale, thrills without damaging your sleep.

But amid the garden grows a tree—

Nobody dies without death's first having seemed beautiful to his imagination. You keep the word from them. You pretend to know nothing. You avoid mention of the shells in the plunge pool rock.

A vision is at once beautiful and cruel—cruel because whatever paradise it promises must be conceivable, must be plausible so as to twist the heart. The Eden of the Animals would have no power over me—except to restore that sweetness before sleep the adult heart loses some of at every waking—if it didn't cry *almost*, if it didn't lie closer with each hour of science, each second of the will's endurance. The fossil in the glacial rock, tuatara in his seacave witness: Everything that was, is; all that's necessary is to get the right combination, the right sequence of genes, one more *whirr* of the engines of desire…one live cell of dimetrodon….

What's necessary? If I knew, I would do it. I would break any rule, defy any god. *Come back!* I'd scream into the dark cave, not caring what came out. I'd stand on the edge of time and with unanswerable longing and vehemence call *Come home! Come home!*

❦

To what ends will the blue goddess Terra go to survive us? Volcanos? Droughts? AIDS? Will she tear her ozone like a silken veil? Will she set the atom in our fists, cover her face, stand back?

The imagination of death is abroad. The rivers run red. The clouds are mushrooms. The pin-up of the age is a starving child squatting over cracked clay. Something must be said to make it seem absurd, unnecessary.

I am not a joiner. My politics are, to put it generously, subtle. But I manage to do something now and then to earn the name of environmentalist. Why that, when the world's suffering offers so many possibilities for concern? Because to hear my children calling heartsick to the gray whale and the condor irretrievably departing is a deeper blow than I wish to weather now. Or ever.

Winter

The first hard wind of autumn around the Great Lakes is called The Witch. The lakemen hate her. She veers in from the northwest with polar ice bunched at her breast, whipping barges into harbor, beaching everything not anchored down. It's everyone's bad time. Boatmen dream of inland farms. The mantis snags a blown leaf with her saw-tooth arms, bites the pointless gold, swiveling her green head toward starvation. Katydids fall onto the walks, fat as green cattle, too stunned to move. Tatter-winged moths cling to the screen door with their last strength. Geese beat southward from the Great Slave, their gray harp wings keening in the moonlight. The princess falls among the dragons.

There is nothing left to fight for.

We are not in our right minds.

Brown leaves flap from the oak branch, crying, *Betrayed*.

❧

I climb the hill to do my laundry in the magical rim-of-the-woods laundromat where I held the ovenbird and will watch a sharp-shinned hawk flutter at eye level from tree to tree, back and forth like a child swinging on columns. Someone left the lights burning and the door ajar, and on the walls moths have gathered by the hundreds, moths of the palest violet, deep purple, white, near-white, gray, chestnut shot with gold, chrysoprase lunas, gigantic polyphemus that would spill over the edges of my hand, all wavering and fluttering like leaves in a jeweled forest. A dragonfly angrily circles the light bulbs. My impulse is to run for my insects guide, but the bounty is too great, and I wouldn't know where to begin. I carry some outside in my hands. Those that have the strength turn and flutter back. Others, falling onto the ground, begin to crawl, over the sidewalk, over the laundry room threshold, across the floor, into the hard light. As I put in my quarters and start the washer, I notice that the jeweled leaves, like the leaves of the forest outside, are falling. Those on the wall still outnumber those on the floor, but the proportion alters moment by moment. They have come here to die.

Finishing, I shut off the light, close the door, leave them to their ceremony.

❧

It's 10 degrees below zero, the sky as brilliant as burnished metal. A friend and I walk the frozen Exeter River, to gain perspectives impossible over liquid, even from a boat. "Frozen" is inadequate; the river is a gray stone slab ten inches thick, polished too glaringly slick to walk on except where blanketed by the preceding night's snow.

Suddenly, in this terrible cold we see movement.

A waterscorpion crawls across the ice, its breath tubes dragged behind, the painstaking Y of persistent interrogation. I kneel to look. My companion crushes the waterscorpion under his boot. Shocked, I rise to confront him. His face burns with the horror. I see now. I'm the monstrous one. I'll look at anything.

❧

There are certain infernal species, like the bishop pine, that can complete their life cycles only in the presence of fire. Thick husks must be charred away, cones must be coaxed open to a chorus of hissing needles. Vast tracks of swampland and savannah require flash fires to clear away the detritus of decades and let the fresh appear. The Everglades would subside into rolling low meadow without the severe cleansing of flame.

I am of the opposite sort, a boreal nature that needs a howling nor'easter and 20 below to come to an understanding with the universe. On bad days I go down to the road and help shoulder my neighbors' subcompacts out of the shallow ditches along Chunns Cove. "Not used to driving in snow," I say in my most clipped Northern. I like to see their pink faces, feel their shoulders pressed against mine under the bumper.

"I'm better at this," I think. "I'm not as cold as you."

This is, however, untrue. Like a fish in a mountain river, it is possible to survive the cold by matching it from within.

❦

When we were kids, father would wait for the first snowfall and drive us to the metropolitan park. This was a necessary undertaking.

Three open fields punctuated the forest. One field was gigantic. It contained a baseball diamond and wore hole-in-a-board toilets and a beautiful black-wood creosote-fragrant picnic shelter on its rim. To stand in the middle was perfect exhibitionism, as anyone in the forest could see you, and unless it was an interior-revealing winter night, you had no thought for them.

Winters you'd sled down Morningview Hill. If you were very skillful or very lucky, or had one of those cruel black-runnered sleds as long as your body that the boys from the junior high got for Christmas, you could glide all the way from Morningview to the shelter, which had removable walls and windows for winter, and within which there were fires and chocolate.

In summer you played baseball.

I hated baseball, and crossing that field brings memories of my confusion and shame when circumstances conspired to place me on a team. But I didn't mind being where baseball was played; it got me outside, it was normal, and I was known to be so bad at it that nobody expected much.

A time-lapse film of the big field through the early sixties would catch me for significant passages of the summers just standing while the game rang around me—hopeless and unheeded, but happy. Confident that no one would throw anything in my direction, I watched stars glimmer out in that deepening blue that seems now always to have been cloudless, watched bats take wing for twilight forays over Alder Pond. If they shouted "Play deep!" I'd edge to the shadow of the trees, stand with my ankles touching the fronds of the mayapples. Mayapples, which some call American mandrake, possessed and dispensed magic, and to touch them with a bare leg conferred power. What kind didn't matter. Nothing to do with baseball.

The second field lay eastward and was medium-sized, too long and narrow for most games, but perfect for church youth picnics. You settled the giant ripple-sided aluminum punch dispenser on the chestnut stump which had been creosoted and preserved as a sylvan *momento mori*. You grilled hot dogs under the trees at the edge of the field. If you were playing late, the gleam of the coals would lead you home. At one end stood the tallest sassafrasses I have ever seen. Generations of kids ripping off their lower branches urged them up until they were the height and girth of the forest trees.

The third field lay northward, almost against the pond, small and round in its circle of chokecherry and oak.

When we were young and the first snow fell, father drove us to the park, and we'd run to the third field, a necessary undertaking. My sister and I had to be first to walk in the new snow. We could be the first in our yard, or in the street, or even in the great baseball field, but only the third field counted. It was tucked out of the way, silent even when the other fields rang with games, compact and mysterious, its opening through the treetops like a portal or the lens of a telescope. You did not barbecue there. You did not play touch football, or anything loud and communal. It was possible to look for it and miss, and miss again until you gave up. We assumed you had to be going there for the right reason to find it at all. Its strangeness and intimacy permitted belief that only your little circle ever ventured there, or ventured at the significant hour. While my father waited at the wood's edge, my sister and I ran to the center, not trampling but cutting evidence of our presence like two tiny booted lasers, ran back, satisfied for winter to commence. To stand there in heavy snowfall—Thanksgiving snowfall, the flakes as big as quarters, striking lashes and cheek with a palpable caress—was to know serenity unavailable elsewhere, serenity strangely heightened by awareness that it was dark and cold and you were far from home.

❦

For a time I moved steadily northward, from Ohio to New York, from New York to New Hampshire. If I went driving, no matter which way I started out I'd find myself crossing the Portsmouth bridge into Maine, headed north along the seal-glad coast. This was a spiritual compulsion. I needed to go north. Something lay there that I wanted. On those occasions when I considered it at all, I realized what one seeks in a landscape made of contrasting bright and shadow, a land naked and dangerous, the track of the wolf weaving with hunger beside your own.

Definition. The primeval clarity. The single first fact glooming like a mount of black marble over snow.

Now I live a thousand miles south and admit I'm confused. There's too much. At least once a week I have to climb Mount Pisgah to stand in the bare sky, dark amid the light, simplifying.

❦

Bob Dolittle introduced me to New York's Morgan State Forest at Thanksgiving. Bob was—is, I suppose, though it's been years since we've met—a gentle man, whose gentleness must have come from somewhere beyond the circumstances of his life. Perhaps the forest. I was glad when he decided he'd rather not go alone anymore. It worked well for me. I lived with tiresome people then, to save money. When Bob came I could shut the door and be gone a whole day, free.

We hiked with gaudy hats, singing filthy songs as we went so the hunters wouldn't mistake us for deer. You do that in the Rockies and Alaska, too, so the grizzlies won't mistake you for deer. Often it would be the two of us, though on fair, bright days we'd pick up Bob's friend Jaime, the painter, so he could look at the bare colors of northern Appalachian winter, and Jaime's girlfriend, Annie, a potter with the imperturbable serenity that seems to come with that craft. The four of us made a din no hunter could mistake.

Jaime was a demon for fire-building, and twice in a hiking day we'd huddle around a fire he'd conjur from snow in five minutes, his artist's hands red and bare to the cold.

Sometimes I drove there myself, usually just to sit with the car engine ticking to cool under the hood, breathing a minute before returning to my duties in the city. The chickadees said hello and goodbye in a single whistle. They call my name at morning and evening in their melancholy descending whole steps. *David. David.* Anyone with two syllables to his name can claim the same.

So, by the time I needed to, I knew where to go. I went alone, packing automatically, without any sense of what would really be necessary. I included two quarts of Canadian whiskey, blankets, my snowshoes, a walking stick Bob found for me along the frozen river. No food, no map or matches, meaning to go hiking but not to come back.

It had been a bad year. Never since have I been young enough to believe it would never get any better, or that I couldn't stand it if it didn't. One can stand anything, an endurance both well and monstrous, though so common in our race it loses what should be its breathtaking effect.

One loses something by accumulating toughness like the bark of a lowland tree. One gains life, loses innocence. One does not automatically assume the ledger balances.

It was beautiful driving into the afternoon of my last day, exhilarated and melancholy at once, like a character in a movie. Everything was a portent. I leaned on the sill of the car window so the sun could whiten the already white hair of my arm. I sang as I drove alone, making sure the songs were minor and stately and old. I had only the poet's regret of not writing it down, of not somehow preserving what would be my only perfect poem.

Lock the car on the forest road, put the keys carefully in my pocket, hating for a dramatic gesture to turn preposterous at the last moment.

Leave the road, hike up and in.

.   .   .

The slope is steep. The best athlete gets winded the first few minutes of hiking deep snow, and I hit the midpoint of the slope before my breath steadies. After that, it's fine. Chickadees call my name in whole steps from the limbs of hemlocks. Late afternoon, the sun bright at my back, not warm, but pouring a blue-white illusion of warmth on the criss-cross of squirrel and titmouse tracks, my own snowshoes galumphing amid them like the slither of a great ice serpent. I fist my hands under my gloves, draw in the fingers to keep warm.

Easy at the top. I relax, spread my legs and move, like a sailor home from the sea, running the high ridge. I remember to use my hips, plowing the snow. Dolphin through water. Merlin midair. I run enough to get warm, but not so much as to sweat, which would chill me again. Deer hate the top, where their silhouettes stand stark against the sky. I like it. I know if I flew from here I would beat out forever and not touch land.

The tracks diminish to a few birds, a few blown fragments of leaves, me.

Bob had showed me if you stop at certain places in winter and whistle, the mountain whistles back. I hit one of those places first try. I stop, whistle. The trees whistle back, though how I don't know. Chimes of ice, a ripe sounding board of shattered wood? Ghosts? Not an echo, but an independent sound, an answer in a different key, with a different urgency, high and glassy. I whistle as I snowshoe, the Answerer trailing me like the Ancient Mariner's ice spirit guiding his ship from the Pole.

The clouds are very high and break just westward, so it begins to snow without the sun's dimming before it sets. I pick a memory from my head. *Soon I will have no memory,* I think, anxious to remember how that feels.

I aim at a hollow under a snag of lumber that might be clear of deep snow even now. It is. A few minutes' scratching about makes it ready. I lie down, snow flying heavy around me now. I unlace my snowshoes, put them outside, for a marker. I pull the blankets from my pack, wrap my feet, settle back.

I arrange the two quarts of Canadian Club on the ground beside me, so the second will be in reach when I'm blind drunk from the first. For some reason I have brought a mirror. I tie that to a stick directly overhead, as though I'd be able to watch my exit in the settling dark.

I'm not an experienced drinker. I didn't know that I'd dislike the taste of whiskey. I sip gingerly, making faces for the benefit of the dark of the snowcave. But I keep at it, sip after sip, until chemical warmth tingles my nose. The need to shift around to get comfortable diminishes. I need to piss, but it's too cold and I can't move, so I let go where I lie. I want to sleep. I mean to sleep. I keep drinking. I feel myself going blank, cheered because I think I've succeeded in drinking the bottle dry.

Sometime—maybe a day—later, waking comes as a dim uneasiness, like a too-hot bath stayed in too long. It's not really a disappointment until I remember why I came. It's neither dark nor bright in my cave, though enough light filters through the snowy roof to show the full whiskey bottle kicked on its side at my boot-tip, the used one still a quarter full, propped on a hillock of snow at my elbow. Not having drained it fills me with limitless melancholy. I know I should cry, but I'm too drunk and too sick. Realizing I'm passing out again is a relief. I go out thinking *This time!*

Then follows a period of alternate waking and sleep. I know I should reach for the bottle to drain it dry, should throw off the blankets, but I'm unable or unwilling to move. I wonder why I haven't frozen in the blizzard. Or perhaps I have. If so, it too is a disappointment.

Dreams unfold incessantly, insistently. I concentrate on them, to see if they are different from the dreams I'm used to, if they are death. In one dream stands a beautiful forest, like that around me, but greened and sweetened by springtime. I have food, crackers that enlarge when removed from the crackerbox to great white cakes the size of baseballs. If I hold them up to the trees, animals begin to crawl from the shadows, golden animals with the habits and dispositions of squirrels, but bird-like in the vividness of their color. Gleaming like little suns, they nibble from my hand. This goes on a long time. When I give them the last of my crackers, I realize my own hunger. Not mere daily hunger, but teeth at my gut, a mule-kick from inside. In the dream I bend over and moan. This was me vomiting against the wall of the snowcave in real time.

Finally in the dream the hunger is so unbearable that I crush the crackerbox to baseball size and hold it aloft as though it were a further cracker. One of the golden animals scampers from the shade. It stretches up from the forest floor, reaches with gentle ape hands for the box. It doesn't seem to recognize the ruse, for it nibbles the crushed box contentedly while I pet it, gently, then boldly, careful to touch every part of its body. I clamp my fingers around its neck. It doesn't move, keeps on nibbling. I squeeze. Still it is oblivious, and its obliviousness infuriates me. I swing it against the trees, whirling left and right until its head explodes. Long arcs of blood fill the air, darken the golden fur. Fury and hunger burn my gut. I bite through fur, spit, bite again, close my teeth on bleeding flesh.

I wake. It is pitch dark. I smell the vomit. I want to sleep, and I begin sinking downward, but a cold fear grows at the back of my mind. Fear becomes conviction. I am not alone in the snowcave.

How long I lie paralyzed with whiskey and sickness and panic I don't know. Eventually a halo of illumination from outside renders the outline of my pack. With infinite stealth I reach in, clutch the cold cylinder of my flashlight, aim at the far corner of the cave, snap it on. Between my knees, touching the flesh under my denims when it moves, is a weasel. Starved in the middle of winter, it is eating my vomit.

I snap off the light, lie back. Let him feed.

My weasel, I say, knowing it isn't, calling it that anyway, to have my way once.

When I wake the final time, a gray light fills the snowcave. Sound from outside announces the fullness of my folly. It's rain. A January thaw. It figures. I say to the weasel tracks on my floor, "Isn't that just how it is?" For a second I feel like laughing.

There's no hangover. I feel dizzy more from hunger than alcoholic insult. I crawl from the snowcave, work nose and fingers and toes to see if they've been frostbitten or nibbled by the weasel. I tie on the snowshoes, repack my pack—frugally bringing with me both the full and the used bottles of whiskey, one that I drank in succeeding months by minuscule increments poured in coffee, one that I gave away, still unopened, when I moved. I shuffle down the mountain which had meant to be my last site on Earth, cold and hungry in a wilderness of rotting snow. Wild with thirst, I scoop watery snow into my mouth. It tastes of moss and clean metal.

My rusty car sits waiting in the valley. I pick notes from under the windshield wipers, notes from forest rangers concerned for the owner of the rusty Toyota. The texts have disintegrated in the rain. I keep them anyway for a long time afterward, ruined paper smeared with blue, marks of someone worried, even if professionally.

I drive from the forest, worrying about fuel—reluctant to stop for gas because I smell so bad—about the rent, about what day it is, small matters sparkling like wine in my consciousness. I unlock my door at dusk on the fourth day since I'd gone to the mountain. I throw my clothes into a corner, shower, sleep real sleep. In the morning I remember that I'm hungry.

I've left the kitchen window open, and the floor's covered by a delicate veil of snow, so even and thin I think the tiles have faded until I touch them with my bare feet.

❦

In the 1890s, George Vanderbilt caused a trail to be blazed from Biltmore House near Asheville to Buck Springs hunting lodge on the slopes of Mount Pisgah, dividing seventeen miles of peerless wilderness over which he reigned uncontested. It is a habit of his family to acquire fiefs and empires; George has outdone them all. You can stand on considerable peaks and see nothing but Vanderbilt land lordly and unbroken in all directions. The trail comes to be called the Shut-In Trail, perhaps because some of it takes the shape of a close green tunnel enclosed by rhododendron thickets, called Hells not because they're unattractive but because if you stray from the path you'll never find your way out. The Shut-In Trail inclines from about 2,000 feet to nearly 5,000, passing through land of spectacular variety—brooding cliffs, verdant near-jungles, ridge backs and bogs and waterfalls, as though constructed by Disney as an eerily lifelike panorama of the Blue Ridge. What grandees passed along the path in its heyday is difficult to say. The forest has forgotten them.

The Shut-In fell on hard times when the estate became public property, and it was severed in several places during the construction of the Blue Ridge Parkway. Recently Boy Scouts and volunteers restored it and now plan extensions that will enable one to walk from Mount Mitchell to the dizzy gaps of Shining Rock Wilderness. It is a masterpiece of unobtrusive utility. Even where it seems to disappear under loam or into the contours of the hills, it lies firmly underfoot, palpable, unlosable, though sometimes quite invisible. Occasionally, at its wildest corners, at night, one proceeds by a sense of the path, moving as though one were a divinity by sheer will that the way be where one is going.

Storms sometime block it with shattered timber after a hard winter. Yet, inevitably, secret ministers armed with chainsaws clear it away, open the path from mountain to mountain. This is my thanks, folks.

This autumn, discovering that I'd walked a fraction of it without knowing what it was, I resolved to walk it all before the New Year. This can be done in one day if one has thirteen or so hours to spend at a throw. I didn't, or pretended I didn't, and walked it piecemeal, from one of its junctions with the Parkway to the next.

Now it's New Year's Eve, early morning, and I have the last four miles to go. Nothing, I say, though topographical maps tell me it's the steepest stretch of all.

I run at first, to make some time. The western sky doesn't look good. I carry my walking stick on whatever side overlooks the abyss, to prong into the mountainside if I start falling. On the first day of my Shut-In adventure, Christmas Day, I found the walking stick mid-path, driven into the ground by its former owner, a gift and a warning. It's a good stick. Whoever left it had found better or wasn't coming back.

As the map warns, it is very steep. I keep running but start sweating, a bad idea on a winter trail. I slow. Spirit drains from my nerves. I go on sheer will. I make perhaps half the distance when a voice inside says, *Go back*. I trot fifty more paces. The voice speaks again, or begins to, but I've gotten the message. I turn back, not running now, as the joy's out of it. I sit on a log and eat my tangerine, toeing the peels under leaves to spare the gray forest the shock of tropical orange. As I suck the juice from my fingers the voice is saying, *Run*. At last, I run. It feels good. It's the right choice. I'm puffing up the last hill before Beaverdam Gap, where I've left my car, when I hear the sound of a police loudspeaker, almost unidentifiable so far from its proper context. Sore now, and cold, I'm walking. The loudspeaker makes me shy and cautious. A police loudspeaker makes criminals of us all. I deer-step over the crown of the hill, see a Parkway Police cruiser idling beside my little silver Ford.

A quick check of my conscience makes it seem safe to return at a trot. The officer waves and says into his radio, "I've got the gray Escort. We're coming down."

I rather like the sound of "The Gray Escort." I may use that for myself one day. Still, I had no plans to come down. I begin to say so, when the officer points west. Fast as a man walking, a bank of black cloud sweeps toward the mountain. Under it, a moving whiteness. Snow. A blizzard. The gray Escort and I roar down the mountain in the gale's teeth, bold because we know we'll be safe. The cop and the voice whispering *Run* have brought us down. We wave jauntily to the officers who guard the swinging gate so I can sweep through, the last car off before they close the Parkway. It is delicious. We Are the Last Ones. Morbidly prudent, I become romantically imperiled only by accident, fodder for the evening news only by settling down to a good book or falling asleep at the wrong moment.

This time, we had been the last.

You are the last. One thing led to another, and before the Race was quite aware, glaciers once more ground their slow thighs into motion. The others left long ago, scurrying south, but you couldn't quite believe it. You stayed. You chained your tires, checked the four-wheel drive, anti-freezed the engine, but you stayed, liking the idea of being last. Now over the town, glittering under starlight like a wall of glass—

—You wake in the night. You've heard the sound far off before. Never so close. The lights flicker, flash back on. But you've been warned. You dress. You run into the knee-deep snow of the front yard. Snow falls so thick at first you don't notice the Glacier, six blocks away, grinding, downhill, southward. Fast. A lone dog barks furiously, backing and snarling as it lurches at his paw-tips. You gather your belongings, realizing that though you'd determined to stay, you'd planned this exit, subconsciously mapping routes, packing the car many times over—

—The sound is the Methodist steeple crashing, a weird lone bleat from the organ before the ice wall swallows them up. The sound is its smooth glide onto Main Street, kissing the wires to oblivion. The lights go out—

—You run into the yard, the snow thigh-deep now, pack a last few things. The lone dog hang-dogs beside you, bravado chilled. You throw out the crock pot and a hamper of old clothes to make room for him. He curls on the front seat, shivering. The house bows forward, pushed from behind by the ice. You hit the road, swerving and slipping despite the chains. You drive. You keep ahead. Your fingers ache from the pressure on the wheel. Finally ahead, a light, at once morning and the rim of the snowclouds. You ease onto the main road, give it gas, startling the dog awake on the seat beside you. You've made it. You were the last. The people who stood all night looking north with worried faces wave as you pass, then turn back north, as though you were not what they expected. You roll down the windows. The air smells of flowers.

❦

My grandmother told me that you can survive exposure to a winter night if you keep dancing. This turns out to be quite true. Whatever you do, don't lie down. Narrow teeth of the starving await what lies down. Move south, move down, but move. Be in a terrible hurry. Blaspheme as though your life depended on it. Raise the heat. In any case, keep dancing.

❦

I've seen the aurora borealis once, from Ithaca, New York, where I had gone to sing Machaut at a festival of ancient music. Six of us crammed in the director's car, cold and exhausted from our labor in the mills of art. When he stopped, we unpacked grumpily, like people getting out to inspect a flat.

He asked, "Is that the aurora?"

I waited before answering, to comb my experience for something else it could be. I did not want to be fooled. It was too important. Blue draperies shivered in the northern sky, stars twinkling behind them. Sometimes the draperies compressed until they were thin streamers, the hair of albinos in deep water. Sometimes they filled the sky, top to bottom, a wall of quaking light.

"Yes," I said, "it is the aurora."

Someone added, "Or nuclear war."

I considered this. It was possible, though Syracuse was all that lay northward, and I doubted that it would go first. As I watched the light, I heard a voice, familiar yet long absent. It was my mother's voice, saying from the back of my brain what she'd said long ago, looking into the same unchanging sky at another vivid and temporary light.

"You will remember this night always."

I looked. Drank it in. I made them wait for me.

Soaring

O f all earth's creatures, only insects possess true wings; that is, wings that were always wings and never forelimbs. Everything else that has ever taken to the air has by some convulsion of genetic will transfigured itself utterly.

Say you are an early Jurassic carnosaur. Your cousins include the greatest terrestrial carnivores of all time, nightmarish *Antrodemus*; bully-boy *Albertosaurus* haunting the foothills of the northern Rockies; that paragon of calamities, *Tyrannosaurus*. You expect the best is over for your clan, not realizing that nature has something in mind for you. It has happened twice before; it will happen once again, but never with such spectacular success. Your DNA takes it into its mind to leap off the face of the planet. It hollows you from within, whittles out your bones until they're empty as whistles, strutted here and there for support. It speeds up your heart, boils your blood, knocks out your teeth, dissolves your tail and fingers, swells your breastbone, tortures your comfy green scales into feathers, and not *one* kind of feather, but down and secondary and gale-defying primary. It miniaturizes, miniaturizes, miniaturizes. It takes away your sense of smell. It forbids live birth to you forever. It sharpens your eyes beyond the power of any lizard; you can spot a beetle on a stone from a thousand feet.

Your earliest fossil, Archaeopteryx, causes a sensation when someone digs it out of a German limestone quarry, for here is evolution's proof in stone, a transitional form, part bird, part reptile. Except that your feathers are perfect. You can fly. You take to the wind one Mesozoic morning, land in my locust tree with grass in your beak for this year's nest. I greet you, stock still behind my window whispering *Cardinal!*, a name you'll take as easily as all the others.

❧

I had a parrot once—actually, a canary-winged parakeet—named Capella, after the star. Aware of her power of flight only in moments of fury or panic, Capella climbed from her cage and walked where she would, crossing whole rooms to bite the toes of people she disliked, or to mount beakhold by beakhold onto the shoulders of the chosen. Often when she was out and about I'd be paying imperfect attention and inadvertently kick her across the room on my way to the refrigerator. When I took the time to contemplate these occurrences, I realized their strangeness. Usually she didn't deign even to squawk—and Capella was a great squawker. She seemed hardly to notice. She righted herself and took off again, jungle-green and undaunted, into whatever mischief she anticipated. Change the scale and you have a sixty-foot giant drop-kicking me half a mile. I believe I would have squawked.

Capella's durability led me to contemplate the skeletons of birds, an engineering triumph to hush the mouths of the prophets, to bring the suicide down from the ledge.

The girdle is a grass leaf dried and curled. Spine's whittled to a splinter, a thorn. Clavicle is a taut hair holding without weight. Everything's reduced, streamlined, punched through with air pockets, honed for flight. Were we as retooled to house our vaunted brains as the bird is for its wings, we would be as ambulating spheres of skull, bulged with eyes, nerve-ropes tasting the air.

Wings are power without mass. They are a folded feather, toothpicks thickened with blood, in good wind flying by themselves.

Girder, crossbeam, strut, willing to bear, made to lift; with that furious heart behind them, lighter than air, nimbler than light, made to hover, veer, power, descend, home in, stoop, evade, ascend. Kick them across the kitchen floor, they gather and leap back. Hurl them into the hurricane, they seize the whirlwind and rise.

Fury is not the cat or the bear, but the wren. Boldness is the chickadee ripping thistles from the bear's coat, snatching grubs—as I have seen them do—beneath the beating ax. Killdeer leaps before fox and wanton boy, dragging her wing away from coming generation. Geese hurl above Everest. Why not higher? The atmosphere thins, refuses to bear. Each day they lie down impossibly midair, take their bit of earth up, insubstantial, indestructible, stop because the world stops, not their will, not their bones.

🦃

Storm comes black and snow-color. Last of winter, intending to be remembered.

It's the worst day of the year, and I mean to run.

I choose carefully. I choose so to bend the wind, this gray scythe mowing from the northwest. Something to hold me down. Shorts, sweatpants, T-shirt, fleecy pullover washed a hundred times, smooth as water. Jacket, wind-shearer, red, so to stand out in the blue and steel-gray warring over the mountain.

Pull on my shoes. Sleet-gripping waffles.

Outside old snow turns to iron, then rusts away. *Get worse*, I say, *I'm coming*.

Out. *One* two, *One* two, a cadence until I calm my breath. Zipper higher around the neck, cap lower, keep in the heat.

On the mountain the storm howls. I climb, holding my right hand over my eyes when the rain cuts. Wind smashes the hilltop oaks until I wish for them the power to lie down. *Yield!* I holler up to them. The words kick back, rolling in my throat. I bend low. I compromise and run.

The storm stands against us. What we've done I don't ask. Endured. Walked out less beautiful than the year before. It has its reasons. Maples crack and slip as I pass. The hollow ones go first. They're losing. Air flows around, thick suddenly, an angry river, a

181

torrent of gray light. It withdraws; it sucks the wood back. Wood is strength; against loss, against subtraction it has no weapon. Limbs burst. Fragments aim for my jacket, the moving red of defiance. We duck and run.

I sense something that's too strong, something that can be gotten around. I smile, holding that knowledge to my chest like a private sun. I bend at the waist, turn my face from the drive of the rain. I go a little the way the tempest wants me. Pushed to a new road, I take it. Make it mine.

The trees see this, hunker down, trying to be me. But they're braced and rooted. The hill plunges down, leaving them alone against the roaring sky. They raise their limbs and wail. Dead leaves cut my cheekbone, whisper of an elder child's last hour.

Whatever the storm does to the mountain, I go my way.

I'll scurry home and put on the kettle. I'll be safe.

Be storm a hammer, I am no anvil.

Be it sickle and flail, I am no field.

I do not stand for it. I leap and run. I tell my feet the epics of hurry, sagas of speed. Faster. The dog wind snarls behind us. The bull wind lowers his black neck to charge. I mark time, waiting, step aside at the final instant. It could come at us all day and we'd have room to run. *Come!* I taunt the locomotive wind. It comes, comes, comes, and I'm not there.

Trees. Poor oak. Sweet, fading fir. Too strong. Too just and vertical. They stand in combat, mortal, musical. I twist to the road again, leap downed lumber, singing goodbye.

When overhead hangs a hawk.

Kestrel, I think, for the little bright of him in dim light. He oars the crest of the mountain, lifts, drops, soars flat out, stoops to the crumpled wood. Hard as wind beats him, he beats back. He holds like blown flame. He stands in wind over the crown of my head, an escort, an angel—whether of vengeance or protection doesn't matter. Tense, terrible, still in that whirling like a rip in heaven.

You! the hawk shouts. I look up. Wings the blades of a wind-knife, cutting.

Hawk transforms me. A moment ago I was a man running in bad weather. Now I am Homo in an allegory, caught between

182

magnitudes, axle between two stillnesses, bird and planet, a messenger who must bear witness between two dangers.

Hawk says, "Nothing you know is quick enough."

Hawk says, "Whatever touches ground is root and fetter."

Hawk sleeps on the wind, taunting and soaring. I have no reply.

I say to my struck-dumb Nikes, *Lift! Lift!* I run harder. Break the spell. Hawk shifts, rides to the next gap of the mountain. I haven't said my piece. I call him back. I wait, but sky stays empty. *Hawk!* I thunder, *consider this—*.

Sleet shuts my mouth. My shoes, my wind-turning jacket take me down into a havoc of sheared branches. Interrupted buds swirl in the sewers. Willows spread their hair across the grass. My limbs are sorry for their pride. The lopped trees bring us to our senses.

From the valley the storm sounds sweet and high. Hymns in the conifers. Twigs and trash come sailing. The storm flails halfway out to sea. I wrap my arms around me. I'm not quick enough to keep off the cold. But I'm all here, fingers and toes, eyes not melted out by visions, arms not feathered by longing to ascend. Running, slow: flame tamed, coals bright in the grate of bones.

I could climb that wind and ride if there were a little less of me. If I were quick enough. A bounding leap from Pisgah, sail into the sky.

But I am strong. Strong enough to make up for it. I pound the thawing earth, break the ice-roof puddles with blows of my feet.

I find a good pace. This will carry me home. I pass through the storm's skirts, laughing upright on the beaten way.

❦

Sitting in a thicket. Spring, before the leaves, a few hepaticas furred and lavender in the glades. I sit very still to watch a grouse strut and peck. It's been a quarter of an hour, and I've seen nearly as much grouse as I need. I stir to get up, when a dark shape shoots through the trees. I crouch, waiting. The wings seem much too wide to slip between trees, but they do. It nears and nears. The grouse must see if I do, but she stands frozen. The shape hovers over her, falls, strikes. A red-tailed hawk. It covers its prey as though I were a rival predator (which I am), rips her to death, clutches, lifts heavily into the air, grouse broken in its claws. I go to the spot. From a spatter of blood I take two feathers.

The grouse I saw go. The hawk must be gone now, unless very, very lucky. I keep two grouse feathers in a wooden box to this day, their shafts brown with what only I know is blood.

❦

I recall when I started bringing all thoughts back to the place where everything is still and cold.

We lived on a farm, in a house overlooking a pond. The pond had been dug for cows, but over the years some fancy of the farmer led him to enlarge it and stock it with exotic waterfowl. When the farmer left, most of the birds left too, one way or the other, except for durable farm geese and a pair of mute swans that beat off all competition, even the foxes that came raiding nests. Canada geese, attracted by the relative safety and calmed by the swans, formed the habit of stopping over during migrations.

Then they began to abide all winter. This was possible because the cornfields round about were sloppily harvested, or perhaps harvested recalling biblical injunctions in favor of gleaners. South-ward, gentleman farms lay in deep fallow all year. Hunters were polite, and I gave permission for deer in order to protect my geese. They were safe unless they threw themselves in the peril of the air, over Windham and Garrettsville where the brush bristled gun barrels.

It was not so far north then, not so cold.

Before Christmas the cold clamped down. One week, two weeks, five days in each when the mercury sank below zero. The snow sang that high cold song it has below zero when I walked between the buildings. My breath made gray sugar on the windows.

On the fifteenth day of it I heard a sound on the pond. The wind comes from that direction, and I hadn't looked there since the weather turned hateful. I rubbed my hand on the rime of the glass until I could see a little. I saw a wild goose on the pond fighting dogs. She didn't move, or just her wings and snake-neck stabbing, her tongue arched like a catapult against the bottom of her beak.

Geese are tough animals. I had my glasses broken and the wind knocked out of me by the blow of a wing. An angry goose can drive off a dog easy, or two if she's mothering.

Four dogs were yapping out on the ice.

I yelled *Fly!* and the window sealed with frozen breath. I ran outside yelling *Fly!* I kept yelling and running until I was on the pond myself. If it could hold a pack of dogs it could hold me. Usually dogs give way to an assertive man. They didn't. They backed from me with terrible slowness, snarling, their paws quivering with indecision, their muzzles drawn back over yellow teeth. They wouldn't give way. They'd drawn blood, and battle fury tingled in their brains.

I saw why the goose didn't fly. Her feet were frozen in the ice. I backed off slowly. I let them have her. They gnawed her down to ankle bones.

The flock settled when the dogs had had their fill and trotted off. They weren't at ease. The pond was a highway any enemy could cross. They gabbled all night, the lone gander honking and squawking out toward the edge. I thought of the one fact I know about them: Geese mate for life. I picked out the gander's high drone from the noise of the flock, monotonous, obsessive. Before morning I got up, took my ax, ran to the pond, sledged the ice, beat open water for them. The bloodied patch swirled in the center, sank.

❦

Sometimes I think I hate them. The wind is a fury, but it bears them, takes them where they will. Takes them home. One snow, two snows, a dozen winters; we have not moved.

❦

I lived in upstate New York. Autumns, wind came for a day or so from the southwest, as though there were a sea there. Each of those days I went hiking between two green lakes left by the glacier. Once I heard a lone goose, a big Canada. I ran to the sound, saw him rolling on one good and one stiff leg. He'd gotten himself too deep in the thickets to try his wings. Blood stained his breast where it met the hurt leg, a few feathers blown away by a shotgun. I shouted

"Fox!" and "Dog!" and "Hunter!" but they didn't move him. I walked close. He rolled to get away. I ran; he ran, hissing. I ran him to the lakeshore, where from under the boughs it was suddenly clear. He beat his wings on the pebbles, on the green water, lifted heavily over the circle of hills, shot off southward without another sound.

❧

I need to tell another tale of the same green lakes. It comes to mind because for several nights a pair of screech owls have shrieked and shivered in the black locust at my window. I say "pair" as a minimal estimation. I haven't actually seen the owls, but I assume that such variety of disturbing noise cannot be made by one and need not require more than two.

The sound is at once pathetic and appalling, like a very tiny monster hoping to frighten you clear of its lair.

When I worked in a liquor store in Syracuse I walked home at night through Thornden Park, a tattered, lovely grassy space that acquired the reputation of being dangerous after dark. Perhaps it was, but one made it a point of macho honor to proceed through at any hour of the day or night, or at least never to be perceived going around. I had done so and had never seen much that looked suspicious. It occurred to me, however, that perhaps I lent a legend to the night, galumphing through by the belt of Orion, a scurrying shadow that could be interpreted from the street as that of a desperado.

But one night the meadow was flakked by searching flashlights, Madison Street below lit with police lights turning blue circles on their turrets.

"What's the matter?" I asked the black space behind one of the flashlights.

"Screaming. Somebody heard screaming up here."

As the officer spoke, he politely held the light away from my eyes. Its ray climbed an ancient box elder, where lined up on a branch like toys on a shelf sat four screech owls. They fluffed and glared and shifted from claw to tiny claw. I stretched my neck to see them better;

they craned and leaned, as though mocking my rude curiosity. I insist that the expression on their flat faces was one of droll conspiracy. Before I could direct the officer's attention upward, the owls glided soundlessly off, one by one.

"Good luck," I said, lacking the heart to tell him whose the screaming was.

Terror of the screech owl's voice diminishes somewhat after one lays eyes on the creature itself. No owl is cuddly, but the small ones are droll, baby-faced, unlikely threats to mammals of our size.

The great owls are another matter. As a child I visited a farm where my father bought dry corn to feed the birds through winter. Across the door of the barn stretched cruciform the white corpse of a shotgunned barn owl, "To keep out rats and sparrows." I thought it could keep out wildcats, with that acre of wing, that dark intensity of eye from heart-shaped visage, formidable even in death.

More intimidating still is the great horned, the Halloween owl that really does say *Who?* with the tone of God on Judgment Day. I've met hunters who claim that great horneds can kill and carry off fawns. I believe it. I have found undigested fox brush in owl pellets, and once the wing of a hawk.

My first great horned appeared years ago, while I played with friends in Goodyear Heights Metropolitan Park in Akron. High in a white oak we spied what we assumed to be a squirrel's nest, and being boys our impulse was to lob sticks at it to provoke some action. It was quite early in spring, and our heavy jackets impeded our throwing arms, but at last I got one high enough to nick the dark shape. The next instant it sprouted wings, and with a sepulchral *Who?* glided from the limb above our astonished heads farther into the deep of the forest. I fell permanently in love.

Years later my relationship with the great horned owl reached a climax that I hope but do not really expect will come again. It was at those green lakes in upstate New York, on a crisp late-autumn day after a spectacular cold snap that had turned the waters of the north to iron. I walked the lake path with my hands jammed into my pockets. The forest stood so utterly bare that every scurrying rodent, every stay-at-home bird shone in blue-white clarity.

Still a way off, I began to scan a brown complication halfway up a tulip poplar tilted over the lake. The mass was out of place on the clean outline of the tree. It reminded me of the "squirrel's nest" of my youth, and I walked faster, hoping for an owl, a tardy migrator, perhaps a ghostly presence from the ultimate north.

A hundred yards off I knew I had an owl, a big one, a great horned, plain as a hillside. I commenced a cautious approach, stepping with a deliberation hard for an impatient man, stopping whenever her head swiveled my way.

Closer.

Closer.

Closer than I'd ever stood before. Nearly as close as I'd ever been to a wild thing. I couldn't believe my luck.

There's a point at which the dream of approaching wild things—touching them, tasting acceptance lost since Adam—wavers over into nightmare. We are men; they are beasts. It is our business to stalk, theirs to flee. We are uncomfortable when it turns out otherwise. By those green lakes one summer I stalked a fox in a sunny meadow, hoping to see his den. After letting me stalk a few hundred yards, he turned and looked at me. Assuming it was over anyway, I approached briskly, waiting for him to scurry. He didn't. I took another step. Another. Fox stayed put. No change of expression on the red muzzle, not even the apparent effort to "freeze." He scratched a flea, surveyed the meadow, no more interested in me than in the white moths circling his head. I'd crept close enough to touch him with my boot when the horrific word *rabies* formed in my brain. I backed off, quicker than I had come.

I don't know that the fox was rabid. I know I needed an excuse to get away from an experience more intense than I wanted.

So my emotion was not pure delight when I touched the base of the owl's tulip and she hadn't budged. I gazed up, hand flat over eyes against the sun and the glare of the lake ice, and saw the owl's legs tangled in wire, and the wire tangled in complications of the tree.

I want to say the decision formed instantly, but it didn't. Her branch extended over imperfectly frozen ice, itself over incalculably deep water. Not a tree climber as a boy, I'm no better at it now. The two miles to my car was a long way to go with soaked clothing or broken bones. Still, one knows what one can live with, what one cannot. I began to climb. I remember nothing of the way up until I reached her limb, began to snake out, cooing ludicrously, *Good bird, good bird.*

I keep saying "she" and "her" without knowing whether I can tell male from female owls. She *looked* feminine, at once, vulnerable and haughty, a princess in durance.

As I inched out she leaned back as far as she could from me, until she must have teetered on her tailbone. Her struggling had wrapped the wire tight, so no matter how she pulled, her feet remained immovably involved. The yellow eyes opened incredibly wide in what was inseparably threat and indignation.

The great horned is a very large bird, a hunter, an exquisitely equipped carnivore. Tyrannosaur flows in her blood. I kept flinching from the peck of the skunk-dismembering beak. It never came. She watched as I worked the wire free, blinking, raising her wings to let the loops of it pass under. I removed my gloves to work more freely, working faster against the paralyzing cold. When I touched her body with my naked hand, a thrill went through me like an electric shock. I imagined slipping my fingers under her feathers for a moment to warm them, but never dared.

The wire dived onto the ice—baling wire, I figured, trying to imagine how she'd picked it up. Maybe mousing in a barn. It made a musical note when it hit. The owl cocked her head to the sound but didn't budge. She sat free a beat before she realized. I kept still with imagining a face full of frenzied owl. We stared at each other from the ends of our branch so long I broke concentration, daydreamed of warmth, caught myself slipping. The motion of my grabbing on startled her. She flapped. Her eyes announced that she felt nothing hold her.

Several things happened at once. The owl took to the air, and though the lift-off was absolutely silent, it startled me so that I lost my grip on the limb, plunging as the owl rose. Between us we achieved a mystical balance, mirror images diverging at equal distances from the same tulip branch. She shot straight up, then veered toward the center of the lake.

I, however, did not change directions. Down and backward, with the sky at the same apparent remoteness no matter how far I fell. The tree hadn't seemed so high when I was on it.

If you hit hard enough you actually do see stars. I felt the pain in my bones, savoring it, testing it to see what was broken. It flowed to full tide, then receded. I gave thanks. All that pain meant that the ice had held. I waited for news to shiver down my nerves from the extremities; as the shock laved away, I knew we were whole and unbroken. I rolled the six or seven feet to shore. As I staggered to my feet, the owl beat onward, visible near the far side of the lake, poised to vanish into owl-colored distance. I watched her disappearing-place for a long time, wanting to holler *Who?*, but afraid somebody would hear me, or that nobody would.

Leviathan

Six feet long, a torpedo of lean silver malice, my first shark emerged on the end of a fisherman's pole from waters where I'd been swimming at Avalon, New Jersey. I asked to touch it, and when I did, I pulled my hand away raw from contact with its emery-board skin. Lodged between two of the shark's teeth was a band of untarnished brass, gleaming in its mouth like a gold gap—a boat fitting, perhaps, bent unrecognizably by the power of the jaws. The fisherman worked it out for salvage. As he did, the fish's head moved slightly, as though to get a better view of the procedure.

I said, "It's still alive."

The man with his hand in its mouth said, "Sure. Will be for an hour or two. Unless—" He took a long knife from his pocket and offered me the honor of eviscerating his catch. I declined. Instead, I stood back, wondering who'd thought of this thing, this hideousness and splendor under one compact skin. Once he had cousins ninety feet long whose gape could admit an automobile. Even today, old great white sharks, which are believed to avoid shores and keep to unnavigated emptinesses of the deep sea, reach unknown sizes, reach unknown spans of years, devour unknown prey.

Maybe I know who. The next question is *why?*

Ad majorem Dei gloriam?

❦

Sea's edge. On the brink of any such immensity I take occasion to rejoice that I am not the Creator. Would I have devised mitochondria? Would diatoms have occurred to me in a hundred billion years? What of the horseshoe crab rotting at my sneaker tip? Where would I have gotten the clue for protective mimickry, for metamorphosis, for the flying snake, the sea-squirt? It would have been a hash, a botch from the word go, a planet knee-deep in gaudy blossoms and snaking Crayola sea-birds, sterile and starving.

It's the artist's pride to think we create. We tinker. Rearrange. This is at once humbling and, when we consider that tinkering and rearranging compose exactly the process of evolution, exalting.

The brass-toothed grin of the shark would never have sprung from me. My imagination encompasses terror all right, but nothing so subtle and efficient.

But, given a night of vast and holy dreams, I think I *might* have hit on the great whales. My imagination tends actually to strength on the mammoth side of things. Sky, mountains—in a roughed-in, unfinished sort of way—might occur to anyone. So might these vast shapes gliding in the deep, secret and blessed, therefore hidden from the eye, therefore insinuating to the heart as no plain thing is.

I might have thought of the great whales. It's sure I think of them now—dream of them, even, in dreams that possess the calm magic of restoration.

❦

I first saw whales in the Atlantic off Portsmouth.

We rose before the sun to arrive timely at the *Viking Queen*. Despite steady September rain, I left my weather gear home, meaning to sail unencumbered. Several dozen people assembled at the wharf. Like me they were wildlife enthusiasts who'd sent in thirty bucks to reserve passage to the empire of the whales. We boarded, checked out one another and the lavaliers of camera and binocular we bore around our necks while The *Viking Queen* slipped into the Piscataqua, chugging toward the sea. Scowling dark men stood spread-legged behind hot-dog cookers, braced and defiant. The doors of the heads banged open with the swells. Faces stiffened around the first squalling child. Yet at the instant the ship lurched into the current, the clouds dissolved and dawn came like a scatter of coins across the water.

The Piscataqua River between Maine and New Hampshire is torn by one of the swiftest tides in America, and our passage from river to sea involved a palpable violence. The outgoing water churned back on itself like a collapsing wall, the slurry presided over by a wheel of gannets.

This being an Audubon tour, we were well supplied—oversupplied, if the truth were known—with superb birders. Black motes on the waves were identified with dizzying dispatch as scoters and ciders, great and double-crested cormorants, two swift merlins disdaining to take harbor in our rigging, loons (both common and—though there was dissension from the verdict—arctic), northern phalarope, a flock of black-bellied plover, gulls so plentiful we sighed with ennui when they flapped in the light of our scopes.

Birding is one of those pursuits requiring an imperial presence. Two good birders can haggle all day over a figure dark and small and too far away, but in the presence of a master everyone goes to school. Fate blessed the *Viking Queen* with two masters. One stood lean and cheekboned in his grave black costume, black cap pulled low over glittering eyes, a dramatic presence stationed on the topmost projection of the ship, scanning all horizons, a portentous mariner, neck festooned with cameras and lenses instead of albatross. The other was an aging, roaring boy, tubby, vivid, the gravedigger to his colleague's Hamlet, braying out the names of birds with hopeful alacrity, willing to be corrected by the other's cautious, "Now, Walt—," the crowd's favorite for his scarlet coat and war stories of bird expeditions past. His percentage of misidentifications was higher than the serious one's, but he made them with suave disregard for mere accuracy, generally without looking, reckoning rather by time and place and knowledge of what *should* be there.

Journeymen made identification coups, or rushed, blinded and headlong, binoculars clamped to their eyes, to whatever side of the ship the action favored.

The sea roughened. The *Viking Queen* rolled sideways into troughs whose crests rose sixteen or twenty feet above her decks—green mountains, translucent, like jade amber hardened around the bodies of fish. Usually prone to seasickness, I was as merry as a child on a carnival ride. I felt insolently well, managing a patronizing smile for those whom necessity compelled to seek a place at the rail.

I believed whatever the bird hierarchy said, dutifully swiveling my binoculars onto the wonders of the northern sea. We were a grim-jawed lot, peering through bent glass, covering all quarters, like archaic coast guards, against the advent of some prodigy.

I did make one sighting on my own: seven ugly feet of shark. To scream *Shark!* seemed somehow more provocative than *Phalarope!*, so I hollered, "Look! Look!" They looked. The fish, besides being huge, came on dark green-gray above, paler below, with a blunt wide visage. It confirmed the impression of stupidity by smacking into the side of our boat, apparently without having seen it. I tallied up the probable number of passengers who'd rather see a shark than a gannet and promoted myself to journeyman wave-watcher.

Despite the beauty of birds and fish, we'd come for whales, and after a few false starts, we saw them.

Archaeocetes—ancient whales—appeared in the Eocene, fully whales, fully adapted to oceanic life. There are no known transitional fossils. Today a pig (or whatever), tomorrow a breaching baleen. I point out this fact because of my love for the swift and catastrophic. I want the mind of evolution to be that of a poet, proceeding by furious inspiration as much as by diligence.

From archaeocetes sprang odontocetes, the toothed whales, including porpoises, dolphins, killer whales, sperm whales and their like. Slightly later appeared the mysticetes—a spectacularly successful group that produced the largest animals ever to exist. Baleen feels like fingernails but is actually analogous to the ridges in the roof of the human mouth. Nature creates thriftily, cobbles with stupefying abandon.

But you know the stats. You've heard again and again how superlatively mammoth the great whales are. One statistic may, however, have escaped notice. The cetaceans have also produced the largest brains that ever existed.

The sperm whale, greatest of planetary carnivores, can hold its breath for an hour, diving to depths of a mile or more in search of squid and other denizens of the benthos, a realm of deep-water blackness and cold that might as well be the dark side of the moon for all we know of it. This whale possesses the largest brain on Earth. Even its species name, macrocephalus, means "huge head." The dinosaurs serve as proof that very large and complicated bodies can be propelled by practically no brain at all. So what does the sperm whale do with all that extra gray matter? It echo-locates, but so do bats with brains the size of beechnuts. Some scientists speculate that it actually stuns or kills prey with high-frequency sonic blasts. That would take maybe another cubic foot of brain. What of the rest? What does the sperm whale *think* about with that superabundance of synapse?

Science—some science, anyhow—now believes that the human brain enlarged as a response to an upright posture. Becoming bipedal left our hands free, and brain, sensing the possibilities, began its imperial progress. Once the habit was acquired, the brain, like a laden cart rolling downhill, kept on in the same direction, getting smarter and smarter, adding jai alai and lace-making to the repertoire of things it could do with its hands—even, with an eye to its own welfare, brain surgery. In the same manner, perhaps, the whale's brain bulked out in order to handle the complicated business of echo-locating. Once started on the path of giganticism, it found no particular reason to stop.

Water can support a body of almost indefinite size, which can contain a brain of almost infinite power and proportion.

So, two giant brains divide the planet, one ruling the land and one ruling, until recently, the water. The labors of the land-dweller we understand, because he leaves *things* behind, books and spearheads and fallen cities. The other leaves nothing. Like Adam in the Garden, he finds a world suited to his needs. He requires nothing further. No walls, no cities, no irrigation ditches, no pyramids affronting the desert stars. In the cetacean *Genesis,* we find Adam unfallen, Eden unforbidden. We find mind without manipulation.

Humankind possesses a constitutional inability to fathom an intelligence that does not manipulate. We rejoice in the toolmaking of our forefathers, calling him *Homo habilis,* Man the Handyman. As I personally find any life a little hollow if it does not include writing along with more public vocations, humans as a race doubt any intelligence that does not—openly and forcefully—assault its environment. How *can* it be intelligent? It doesn't *do* anything.

There are, however, voices of correction. The post-Platonic Greek philosopher Xenophanes, weary of anthropomorphic golden-boy gods, postulated a deity of pure mind, unmoved, moving what He moves through the power of thought. Many intellectual faiths have since come to the same conclusion, that God is best conceived as a nonmanipulating spirit, a holy telekinetic, a radiating Buddha-mind. Whale is the nearest to that this planet comes.

❦

You are the Martian scientist, resolved to try the third planet once again. This time, you listen. From the land you hear, yes, snatches of Mozart, tatters of Euripedes, but mostly a din of sweaty, pointless ferment centered on moving commodities from one place to another, changing the names of those who own them until they rot or rust or pass violently to oblivion.

From the sea—and this surprises you, as you've *seen* nothing that would lead your curiosity down and in—arises a deep music, a hymn of abyss and sea-mount, a chronicle of a million generations in rolling Eden, nothing to do between meals and mating but to think … think…think…. You listen, astonished. A counterpoint of philosophies. Stellar speculations. A flowing, incomprehensible majesty. You board your spaceships. You put on holy dread. You aim toward the great blue blank of the waters.

❦

Saint Brendan, in his famous voyage to the New World, stood in the prow of his boat and sermonized to the sea-beasts. His friends mocked him. The saint's reply is not recorded, but perhaps he answered,

"They, at least, are listening."

❦

My window stands open on the spring night. Frogs call in the bogs across Chunns Cove. They are in love. Theirs is the world's first voice. The whales returned that voice to the waters.

We don't know what the whale sings. Chapter, verse: so much noise. We don't know that we can detect all the song, much less fathom it. We do know that more than one intelligence inhabits this planet. There may be scores of them, and prejudicial perceptions prevent our knowing. Time was the status of women or Japanese as fully intelligent beings could be discussed with straight faces in the academies of Europe. Are we certain that the redwood, the mountain, the rainbow do not send up psalms of thanksgiving for their brief or well-nigh eternal lives?

At the end of *The Marriage of Heaven and Hell,* William Blake writes:

> *How do you know but ev'ry Bird*
> *that cuts the airy way,*
> *Is an immense world of delight,*
> *clos'd by your senses five?*

Walt Whitman thought the grass so many uttering tongues. Why stop at the grass? Isaiah heard the hills clap their hands.

I am convinced in my inward moments that the hymn of the dinosaurs was as imponderably lovely in the Ear of God as that of man, and that His grief in its passing is eternal and unassuagable. These things cannot be said aloud.

❦

Ezekiel's air-lifted to the field of dry bones. One more scene and an epic's in the can. A crane hoists the director into midair. The cameras whirr. The voice-over booms, *Can these bones live?* The crew bends over, laughing. Ezekiel too. They'll need another take. But Ezekiel stops, his face unreadable, astounded. Extends his hand. *Thou knowest, Lord.* He is dancing. Eyes widen. Jaws drop. Bones take flesh around them. Hair shimmers on the wind. Brightness over new skin. Dead voices singing. An old man on the desert lifts his stiff knees, beats his thin arms in air. Ezekiel dances. They drop their gear and run.

&

That things are *things* is a narrow Western prejudice, in the eyes of most world cultures obviously convenient but nevertheless preposterous and destructive. The common wisdom of the planet has been that every thing is a fold of the great Veil, a gesture of the cosmic Dancer, one of so many myriad apples of the eye of the Creator, none of itself more precious than another. Like a mother, the Creator cherishes her children equally, or at best according to a set of preferences beyond our understanding, and perhaps not to our liking.

Amoeba warbling in its drop may be music equal in the cosmic Ear to ours, or the whale's. Still, I don't necessarily want to know about it. I seek enlightenment, but bear with me a midwestern sense of proportion.

I'd put a "Nuke the Whales" bumper sticker on my car before "Save the Whales," to tweak the noses of the righteous.

They remain, nevertheless, righteous.

&

In the event, we saw whales off the coast of New England, fin whales first.

Fin-back whales reach lengths exceeding seventy feet, weigh eighty tons, and live up to one hundred years. They're an oddity in the animal world in being asymmetrically colored, the right side of their jaw and baleen being white and the left side dark. Some believe that this is so the fin can swim in tighter and tighter circles, concentrating its prey, which tries to avoid the white patch, in a little ball that can be lunged at and swallowed in one gulp.

Our fins emerged by the ship, one near enough to be touched by a broom handle. I had never seen a whale before; even with the writer's loathing of cliché, I must report the material truth that it took my breath away.

Before the riders of the *Viking Queen* recovered from the fin whales, someone sighted humpbacks toward Plum Island, breaching and waving their flippers like the canvas of white sailboats. For several hours we followed the whales, which seemed not so much welcoming as lordly oblivious of human presence.

Land creatures wandered the water around us. A bluejay beat furiously past our bow toward Appledore. Butterflies hovered between us and the sun, perhaps blown out by the wind, perhaps arriving by will and on missions of their own. When the great fin whales sounded, they left behind them on the surface of the ocean pools of smooth water, as calm as a garden pond.

Over one of these settles a red butterfly, easing down as though to drink at the pool, as though the sea were an infinite green flower. He touches the surface light as only he can, slams his wings tight behind him and sinks, his descending scarlet visible for an instant under green marble, following down the vortex of Leviathan.

❦

Whales have a trick called spyhopping, which is basically sticking one's head above the water and having a look around. Whale eyesight is not good, but they see essentially what we do: the outlines of continents, rainbow, ships, gulls, moon and stars. Whether they remember their ancient lives on land is unknowable. That they have no regrets is beyond doubt.

Vision

F irst vision is not inevitably best vision, but it remains *first*, a special instance, a grace seldom asked for, seldom repeated.

On the Isle of Man it was a tradition that one, leaving the house at morning, would take as his spiritual guide the first thing his eyes lit upon.

The temptation would be to take control, to squeeze your lids shut and run to the sea, wait to hear the lowing of the whales even if it took a day or a week, to listen for the rustle of ravens' wings over the roof, to walk out and stare straight up into the blank blue of the sky, featureless and infinite.

But one is meant to accept the hazard. Last night's earthworm dried in the sun. The rat in the corn crib. The god at the garden gate.

I paid special attention this morning when walking from my front door just before light. There, in the dewy grass, a young rabbit fed, stopping to kick midair from time to time for sheer joy. I took that as the image of my day. I might have done better. I might not.

I write down firsts—the first flower, first bird, first winter night alone on the mountain—to mark the moment when flower, bird, mountain night announced themselves to the soul, bristling and stupendous with power, almost empty of meaning unless I hammer and sweat to give them shape. That it is necessarily a false—or incomplete—shape might not matter. We'll see.

Bracing and immaculate, first vision takes our breath away without leaving us the wiser. I have a secret for you. I don't want to be wiser. I want to see.

❦

Friends take me caving. I've never been before, and though I'm frightened, I know I fear the idea rather than the cave itself. Sure enough, when I arrive at the cavemouth I am neither apprehensive nor eager but calm, possessing the absurd yet inescapable conviction that I have been here before.

We enter the cave from the north. There are two sounds. Water is one. Flowing water. I listen a long time before recognizing that the other is the drone of bees. The water comes both from outside and from farther down. The bees, moling in from above, lay their honey down in living rock. If we let consciousness lapse for a second, their sound merges with the sound of the water and the impalpable reverberation of the cave to make one sound, an uttered syllable invariable and continuous.

Beyond the reach of our flashlights I expected black. It is, however, purple. We aim the lamps outward, pretending to look for blocks or passages but looking at the purple. Purple like the robe of someone leading us just out of sight. I don't think I've seen purple before. Beside this, every shade is smoky or watery. This is a radiant cold jewel, the mother of porphyry. A dark fire that continues without consuming.

"How do you feel?" my friend asks, remembering that I had been nervous.

"Fine," I say.

I mean, "Welcome."

At what seems to be the bottom lies a clear pool. I dip my hand in. Under the water my hand takes on the color of stone, pale, clean, animate, and impervious.

At this moment I am frightened, and at home.

❧

In Exeter, New Hampshire, I endured my first earthquake. It wasn't much of one, yet it was plenty. I had slept through tremors that had shaken Boston the night before and assumed my chance was gone. But that evening, sitting on my living-room floor reading, I heard a far-off rumble. The floor shook slightly, and at the end of the shaking came a single musical note of incomparable depth and purity. My bones thrilled. My body had become the tone's conduit, like an inverse lightning rod, like the bass pipe of an organ stretching to the center of the earth.

If I'd opened my mouth at that instant, out would have come the Earth's song, bursting the windows onto Mrs. Ledford's black cats on the lawn below.

❧

We've driven all day, and we arrive nowhere. More particularly, we've driven all day to arrive at a reservoir in Oklahoma, flat silver under a flat evening sky. The road has been long, the destination not always sure. At times like this you wonder why you shut your own front door behind you.

Temporarily fed up with my traveling companions, I elect to take my cot outside and sleep under the stars. I mention only the stars to them, knowing they're as relieved to be rid of me tonight as I am to be rid of. Like a caddis fly I subside into my tube and sleep. Around us twinkle the lights of threescore other lakeside campsites, as crowded as houses in a suburb. I doze off to the hum of radios and conversation, comforting under the immensity of night.

One sleeping outside wakes when the sun does. The exposed tip of my nose aches with cold. I notice the strangeness of the light long before it occurs to me to stick my head out of the sleeping bag to investigate. There's an extra brightness, a shade of organic silver that I don't think is produced by dawn glancing off the reservoir waters. Finally, I bestir myself to look.

The lakeshore, the grass and gravel, our tent, all the tents and trailers around us shimmer silver—not metallic, but living, shivering like the garments of dancers. One color from horizon to horizon, silver, lake silver, white rising sun, wisps of fog from the water, the dew, the silver satins of the tents.

I focus and see that the silver is made of tens of millions of mayflies, vibrating their silver wings in the dawn breeze, emerging from their larval stage in the lake, like little gods transfigured in the morning light. A plain of living silver. My sleeping bag bristles with life, pronged and studded with jelling mayflies. I don't like insects near me any better than the next person, but this morning is not one in which to shake them away, but one in which to watch, hardly daring to breathe, certainly not daring to reach and touch.

The sun mounts; their wings dry, and in silver clouds they lift and depart, almost silent, wave after wave. I feel the weight on my knees diminish as my mayflies leap into the air. The last waves are still launching when my friends wake.

I say, "I saw—"

They say, "What?"

I point to the ebbing tide of mayflies. They agree it's a beautiful sight. I am unable to say what fraction this beauty is of the splendor of the hour before. It would be cruel to try. It would be, literally, unbelievable.

We crush a thousand, breaking camp, packing, taking to the dusty road.

I tally these things over and over, recognizing that I might never have seen them. Each time is the first time. A gift, a grace.

❧

December in Syracuse. My heart, faulty since birth, is giving way. Sick constantly, I walk like an old man, bent over, taking stairs with my hands on my knees. The glass ornaments on the Christmas tree remind me of myself, fragile, inconsequential, ready to be put into the box so other people's lives can continue. I live with strangers, afraid to go home lest that look too soon like defeat. I peer from the door New Year's morning, and the first thing, the only thing, visible is snow.

May. After a painful cardiac catheterization, the young, red-haired doctor tells me that the pressure in the chamber beyond the constriction is seventy times normal.

"How did you stay alive?" he asks.

I answer, "Ignorance."

June. This doctor is brusque, middle-aged, seen-it-all. I figure he'll give me the truth. I say, "What are the odds?"

"You're pretty sick."

"What are the odds?"

"Sixty–forty—against."

Incredibly, I am comforted.

Early July. They put me in a room with a man named Tom. He doesn't smoke, doesn't drink, is thirty-two, has had seven heart attacks. He is kind to me, explaining how he's been through all this before and it's really quite routine. His wife, Darlene, brings me ice cream. He rubs my back, his hands so weak I can hardly feel it, but I tell him it is wonderful. As they wheel him out for his second surgery, he says, "Be willing to lose every battle but the last."

That evening Darlene comes weeping to the room to gather his things. I cannot bear to ask. I know.

They come for me the next morning.

Early July. I stand at the hospital window, one hand over the fire in my chest, the other dragging the IV stand along behind. The window opens on a vista of Lake Erie. Over the lake from Canada roars a great thunderstorm, dark at the top, flashing fire at the bottom, stabbing the lake waters, frilling waves against the white sides of the tied-up boats. It hits the window like a gray bomb, rattling the glass in the frame. I stand my ground. If it thinks I am intimidated, it is wrong. I finger the black stitches on my chest.

Suddenly I lift my hand away, hold the wound like Medusa's head before me, to freeze the storm in perfect fire.

Late July. I stand at the edge of the forest with my right hand over the wires that bind my breastbone. At twenty-five, I have finally had the heart surgery prophesied years before. Waking in the recovery room, I said to the surgeon in the husky voice of a throat from which respirator tubes had just been withdrawn, "What can I do now?"

"What do you mean?"

"Can I play tennis? Climb mountains?"

"Anything."

"What do you mean 'anything'?"

"I mean anything. If it doesn't hurt, do it."

I lay back on the pillow. It was what I meant to hear.

I return home and convalesce long enough to draw suspicion away from my real design. Encouraged by my progress, my family takes an afternoon away. I seize the chance.

I walk slowly to the metropolitan park and stand at the edge of the northern meadow. The incision still gives me pain when I twist or pound, so I hold it tight, meaning to twist and pound no matter what. I begin to run. This does not sound remarkable until I remind you that I have never run more than a few dozen yards in my life. I pick an obscure path on a weekday, so no one sees my absurd bent-over posture and the baby steps I have to take against the pain. I scan for onlookers. I'm alone. I shuffle. Then a fast shuffle. A trot. A jog. I press my chest tighter and run. Sweat stings the scar. The muscles of my leg tingle, wondering what has come upon them.

Heart, that red and azure I saw long ago on the doctor's glass desk top, feels new strength. It leaps. It cries out, amazed. It says, *Run! run!* I obey. We are flying under the low branches of the pines, across the blazing south meadow, into the oaks, across the Meadow of the First Snow, toward the glacial remnant of Alder Pond. We've run two miles. Bone, muscle collapse, though heart cries to run. It can't get enough. I sag down on the water's edge, listening to it singing, *Run.*

The wild rose runs to the water. The pond lies silver in the light. Its mallards bob, folded in glare like glass set in diamond. I turn back to the forest, my eyes dazzled with rose-white and water-pale. I run, hand pressed to breast-bone. We do not turn aside. We keep moving.

❦

Index